Better Homes and Gardens®

halloween fun

101 ideas to get in the spirit!

Better Homes and Gardens® Books
Des Moines, Iowa

Better Homes and Gardens® Books
An Imprint of Meredith® Books

Halloween Fun

Editor: Carol Field Dahlstrom
Technical Editor: Susan M. Banker
Graphic Designer: Angela Haupert Hoogensen
Copy Chief: Terri Fredrickson
 Managers, Book Production: Pam Kvitne,
  Marjorie J. Schenkelberg
Contributing Copy Editor: Arianna McKinney
Contributing Proofreaders: Karen Grossman,
  Mary Heaton, Colleen Johnson
Technical Illustrator: Chris Neubauer Graphics, Inc.
Electronic Production Coordinator: Paula Forest
Editorial and Design Assistants: Judy Bailey,
  Mary Lee Gavin, Karen Schirm

Meredith® Books
Editor in Chief: James D. Blume
Design Director: Matt Strelecki
Managing Editor: Gregory H. Kayko

Director, Retail Sales and Marketing: Terry Unsworth
Director, Sales, Special Markets: Rita McMullen
Director, Sales, Premiums: Michael A. Peterson
Director, Sales, Retail: Tom Wierzbicki
Director, Book Marketing: Brad Elmitt
Director, Operations: George A. Susral
Director, Production: Douglas M. Johnston

Vice President, General Manager: Jamie L. Martin

Better Homes and Gardens® Magazine
Editor in Chief: Jean LemMon
Executive Food Editor: Nancy Byal

Meredith Publishing Group
President, Publishing Group: Stephen M. Lacy
Vice President, Finance and Administration:
  Max Runciman

Meredith Corporation
Chairman and Chief Executive Officer: William T. Kerr

Chairman of the Executive Committee: E. T. Meredith III

All of us at Better Homes and Gardens® Books are
dedicated to providing you with information and
ideas to create beautiful and useful projects.
We welcome your comments and suggestions.
Write to us at: Better Homes and Gardens Books,
Crafts Editorial Department, 1716 Locust Street—
LN112, Des Moines, IA 50309-3023.

If you would like to purchase any of our books,
check wherever quality books are sold.
Visit us online at bhg.com.

Library of Congress Catalog Control Number:
2001130191
ISBN: 0-696-21388-5

Cover: Cookie Design—Jennifer Petersen;
  Photographer—Andy Lyons

Permission to photocopy patterns and create
projects for individual use and sale is granted from
Better Homes and Gardens® Books.

Our seal assures you that every
recipe in *Halloween Fun* has been
tested in the Better Homes and
Gardens® Test Kitchen. This means
that each recipe is practical and
reliable, and meets our high
standards of taste appeal. We guarantee your
satisfaction with this book for as long as you own it.

halloween fun

The perfect pumpkins are picked, talk of costumes is in the air, the treat basket is brimming with sweets—it must be Halloween!

Since childhood I've always looked forward to the end of October as a time of unbridled fun. Whether I'm standing at the door to greet lurking trick-or-treaters, throwing a party for fiendish friends, or trimming the house with eerie decorations, Halloween is always a great time at our house.

To help you and your family celebrate the holiday, we've put together a cauldron of ideas to start you off in spooky style. You'll discover grand new ways to transform your home into a creepy castle fit for even the pickiest witch. You'll get secret recipes to tempt all your little ghouls and goblins. And you'll enjoy wonderful party and costume ideas that will start Halloween off with a shriek. So much fun awaits!

So come along and make this Halloween one that you and your little tricksters will remember forever. It doesn't matter if you're 4 or 64, something magical happens when you slip into costume to celebrate the silliest, scariest, craziest holiday of the year.

Carol Field Dahlstrom

contents

Join us in making this Halloween one that will be long remembered, with fun surprises for all your favorite ghouls and boys.

chapter 1

scare them silly

chapter 2

carve and paint them

chapter 3

treat them right

goodies for the ghostly group

Like magic, you can brew up these delicious concoctions for party guests or your own cackling crew.

Page 78

chapter 4

dress them up

spook-tacular costumes galore

From walking trees to smiling flowers, dancing milk shakes to bigger-than-life birds, these unique costumes are sure to be crowd pleasers.

Page 98

chapter 5

get ready to celebrate

party ideas to concoct some fun

Friends and family will sing your praises when you treat them to an unforgettable party filled with ghostly games and not-so-scary fun.

Page 124

scare them

Silly

decorations to spook them out

ghostly light bearer

This gauze ghost will get every Halloween party off to a spooky start. The "boo-tiful" thing about him is that the shape beneath his robe is created from a recycled bottle and lightbulb.

supplies

- 16-oz. clear, plastic soda or water bottle
- Pebbles or sand
- Armature wire
- Wire cutters
- Old lightbulb
- Tape; two 1½-inch wood disks
- Acrylic paints in white and black
- Paintbrush
- Disposable bowl
- Plaster
- Cheesecloth
- Scissors
- Matte sealer
- 2 votive candles
- Gold glitter paint pen

what to do

1 Remove the label from the bottle. Wash and dry the bottle. Place 2 inches of pebbles or sand in the bottom of the bottle for weight.

2 Cut a piece of armature wire 20 inches long. Center the wire around the neck of bottle and wrap once to secure. Make a loop on each end, shaping to hold the wood disks as shown in Photo 1, *left*.

3 Insert an old lightbulb into the opening. Tape the lightbulb firmly in place as shown in Photo 2.

4 Paint the disks white. Let dry.

5 Mix a small amount of plaster in the bowl. Mix it to the consistency of thick paint. Cut four or five lengths of cheesecloth to drape over the frame. Dip a piece in the plaster as shown in Photo 3. Squeeze out the excess and shape over ghost frame as shown in Photo 4. Continue draping pieces over frame, shaping as a ghost.

6 While wet, press a wood disk into each cloth-covered loop. Let dry. Paint ghost with sealer. Let dry. Paint facial features black. Let dry.

7 Paint stripes on votive candles using paint pen. Let dry. Place a candle in each ghost hand.

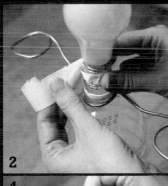

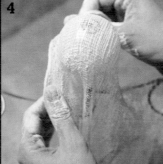

1 2 3 4

Black wire baskets transform into Halloween accents when trimmed with a band of clay candy corn. Use the decorations as candleholders or as candy dishes to keep treats on hand for little tricksters.

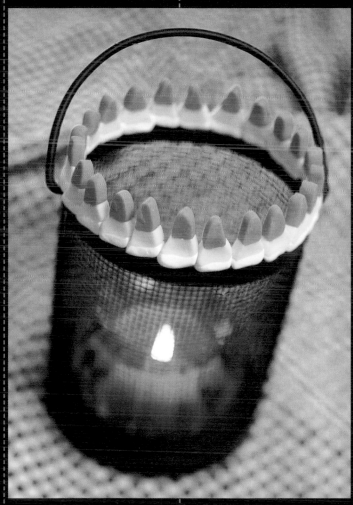

supplies

White, yellow, and orange polymer clay, such as Sculpey
Crafts knife
Black wire basket or bowl

what to do

1 Work the clay in your hands to make it warm and pliable. Roll each color of clay into a long rope. The white clay should be approximately ½ inch wide and the yellow and orange clay slightly thinner.

2 Gently flatten both the white and the yellow ropes by pressing your finger down the length of each rope.

3 Place the yellow rope over the white, joining them with slight pressure. Pinch the top of the orange rope to make it triangular in shape and then press the flat bottom side on top of the yellow rope.

4 Cut ¼-inch slices off the finished roll. Each slice will need to be smoothed and finished by pinching the outside edges with your fingertips to look like candy corn. Firmly press the white bottom of the finished candy corn onto the rim of the container. Bake the clay-topped basket according to the clay manufacturer's directions. Use caution with the finished piece. Although the clay is hardened, it can chip.

boo-tiful photo album

Capture the fun your little trick-or-treaters stir up every Halloween in a photo album made just for the occasion!

supplies

Ruler
Felts in yellow-orange, orange, black, lime green, and purple
Pinking shears
Scissors
Sewing needle
Alphabet beads (1 B, 2 Os)
Small seed beads in clear and black iridescent
Thread in black and white
Large black seed beads
5×6$\frac{3}{4}$-inch (or other desired size) fabric-covered photo album
Fabric glue

what to do

1. Using pinking shears, cut a $\frac{3}{4}$×2-inch piece from purple felt. Use scissors to cut a 1$\frac{1}{4}$×2$\frac{1}{2}$-inch piece from black. Place the purple felt piece in the center of the black piece. Sew the layers together by sewing the letters in place to spell the word boo.

2. Using pinking shears, cut a 2$\frac{1}{4}$×3$\frac{1}{2}$-inch piece from lime green. Layer the boo piece atop the lime green. Sew the layers together by sewing small black seed beads on the black rectangle.

3. Using pinking shears, cut a 2$\frac{1}{2}$×4-inch piece from black. Layer the boo piece atop the black. Sew the layers together by sewing long black stitches extending from the black rectangle outward onto the green felt.

4. Using pinking shears, cut a 4$\frac{3}{4}$×5$\frac{3}{4}$-inch piece from orange. Layer the boo piece atop the orange. Sew the layers together by sewing small black seed beads on the black rectangle.

5. Using pinking shears, cut the yellow-orange piece of felt to fit the photo album. To fit this album, the yellow-orange piece was cut to measure 4$\frac{3}{4}$×6$\frac{1}{8}$ inches, allowing the felt to extend on the sides only. Layer the boo piece atop the yellow-orange felt. Sew the layers together by sewing large black and small clear seed beads on the orange rectangle.

6. Use fabric glue to glue the felt piece atop the photo album cover. Let the glue dry.

black cat jar

A sneaky black cat guards these sweet treats, so take one if you dare! Here, we used a cracker jar, but any large clear glass container will work as long as it has a smooth surface.

supplies
Large clear glass jar with lid
Tracing paper
Pencil; scissors
Tape
Glass paints in black, white, red, orange, purple, and green
Paintbrush
Medium-point black permanent marking pen

what to do

1 Wash and dry the jar and lid. Avoid touching the areas to be painted.

2 Trace the pattern, *below*. Trim the pattern close to the pencil marks. Tape the pattern inside the jar where the design is desired.

3 Using black paint, paint in the cat shape using the pattern as a guide. Let the paint dry. Remove the pattern.

4 Outline the cat using white paint. Add face details. To make small dots for the eyes, dip the handle of a paintbrush into paint and dot onto the surface. Use this technique to make the collar with orange paint. Let the paint dry.

5 Paint alternating green and purple dotted lines around the cat, making a square. Let dry. Add polka dots by dipping the eraser of a pencil into paint and dotting onto the surface. Let dry. Add smaller dots in the centers using the handle of a paintbrush dipped in paint. Let dry.

6 Paint the jar lid orange. Let dry. Paint a large black swirl in the center of the lid. Let dry. Bake the pieces in the oven if instructed by the paint manufacturer. Using a permanent marking pen, write Happy Halloween or another desired message around the edge of the lid top. Add a tiny dot between each phrase.

BLACK CAT JAR PATTERN

It's eerie! It's scary! It's the perfect centerpiece for Halloween! Some spray paint and ghoulish glitter leave their fiendish marks on these flea market finds. Arrange the items on an ornate silver tray, and you're ready to spook the masks off everyone at your next gruesome gala.

supplies

Old vases, candleholders, ornate trays and picture frames, metal bowls with handles, pieces of chain, etc.
Newspapers
Spray paint in pewter and black
Decoupage medium
Paintbrush
Glitter in black and silver
Silver candles
Dry ice

what to do

1 In a ventilated work area, place items to be painted on newspapers. Spray-paint the items black. If painting a frame such as the oval one, *left,* first remove the glass. Paint one side of the glass. Let dry. Spray the items with pewter paint, allowing some of the black to show through. Let dry. Reassemble the frame. The one shown here has a pattern in the center created by the plastic backing piece showing through the glass. If your frame does not have this type of backing, cut and insert a piece of plastic canvas to achieve the effect.

2 Paint decoupage medium on the areas where glitter is desired. Sprinkle glitters onto the wet decoupage medium. Let dry. Shake off excess.

3 Arrange items on tray, adding candles and dry ice as desired.

Caution: Dry ice can cause severe burns. Always wear gloves when handling dry ice.

FISHBOWL
FLOWERPOT

FISHY
FISHBOWL

BEWARE
TREAT HOLDER

fiendish fish-bowls

Whether you like to decoupage, paint, or simply decorate, these clever fishbowls are so easy to make, you can whip up one before a ghost can say boo! Use them to hold Halloween candy or an unexpected treat, such as goldfish or a seasonal plant. Turn the page for the instructions.

fishbowl flowerpot

supplies

8-inch-high round
  fishbowl
Crepe paper
  streamers in
  orange, yellow,
  and black
Pinking shears
Glossy
  decoupage
  medium
Paintbrush
Black glass paint
Pencil with round
  eraser
Three black
  chenille stems
Pony beads in
  black, yellow,
  and orange

what to do

1 Wash and dry the fishbowl. Cut the streamers into squares and strips using pinking shears. Cut one-third of each roll to start.

2 Working on small sections at a time, paint decoupage medium on the inside of the fishbowl. Press crepe paper pieces onto decoupage medium and smooth out with a paintbrush. Change colors and overlap pieces as desired. When the entire inside of the fishbowl is covered with crepe paper pieces, apply a coat of decoupage medium over the entire inside surface. Let dry.

3 To add black polka dots to the outside of the fishbowl, dip the eraser of a pencil into paint and dot onto the surface. Let dry.

4 Twist the ends of the chenille stems together to form a longer piece. Thread a black pony bead on one end and twist the chenille stem to secure it. Continue adding pony beads, alternating the orange and yellow with black. Secure a black bead on the end. Wrap the beaded piece around the top of the fishbowl and twist to secure.

5 Set a potted plant in the fishbowl planter.

fishy fishbowl

supplies

6-inch-high
  fishbowl
Glass paint in
  orange and black
Pencil with round
  eraser
Chenille stems in
  black, orange,
  purple, and lime
  green
2 jack-o'-lantern
  jingle bells

what to do

1 Wash and dry the fishbowl. Avoid touching the areas to be painted. To add polka dots, dip the eraser of the pencil into paint and dot onto the surface.

Wash off the eraser before changing colors. Let the paint dry. Bake the painted piece in the oven if instructed by the paint manufacturer.

2 To make the chenille stem "beads," wrap each chenille stem tightly around a pencil. Remove pencil. You will need approximately 13 black "beads" and 4 of each other color.

3 Twist three black chenille stems together to make a longer piece. Insert one end through the loop in a jingle bell. Twist to secure. Beginning with a black chenille stem "bead," thread it onto the straight piece. Continue threading on "beads," alternating the colors with black. End with black and attach the remaining jingle bell.

4 Wrap the beaded length around the top of the fishbowl. Twist to secure, leaving 6 beads on each tail. Twist tails to form a bow as shown in the photo, *opposite*.

beware treat holder

supplies

Fishbowl
Black vinyl adhesive lettering
Thick white crafts glue
Plastic spiders in orange and black
Artificial spiderweb
Rubber band
24-inch-long piece of ¼-inch-wide orange ribbon
Scissors

what to do

1 Wash and dry the fishbowl.

2 Using small adhesive letters, spell out Take One If You Dare across the top front of the fishbowl, curving as necessary. Spell Boo! at the bottom front. Use large letters to spell Beware across the center of the fishbowl front.

3 Glue a spider inside the fishbowl next to the word Boo. Let dry.

4 Use a small piece of web and wrap it around the fishbowl. Place a rubber band around the rim to hold web in place. Trim the excess from the top. Tie a ribbon around the rim. Place spiders in the web as desired.

This Halloween greeting is as friendly as the smile on the jack-o'-lantern's face. Made from colorful felt outlined with glitter fabric paint, the banner sports a wide rickrack edging.

boo banner

supplies
Tracing paper
Pencil; scissors
13½×23-inch
  piece of purple
  felt
Felt squares in
  lavender,
  orange, white,
  green, and
  yellow
Fusible
  interfacing
Pinking shears
Glitter fabric
  paint pen
Gems in purple
  and yellow
Fabric glue
Wide yellow
  rickrack
Wood glue
Two 1½-inch
  wood doll heads
18-inch-long
  piece of 1-inch
  dowel
Lime green
  acrylic paint
Paintbrush
Yardstick
Orange ribbon

what to do

1 Enlarge and trace the pattern pieces, *pages 24–25.* Cut out. Trace around the pattern pieces on the corresponding colors of felt and on the fusible interfacing. Cut out all pieces. Cut strips of lavender felt with pinking shears for the edge trim.

2 According to the product instructions, iron the interfacing onto the felt pieces, keeping the paper backing on one side. Remove paper after ironing. Using the photo, *opposite,* as a guide, arrange the felt pieces on the purple background. Iron in place and let cool.

3 Outline the letters and shapes with glitter paint; let dry. To add gems in a random pattern, squirt a pea-size ball of glitter paint onto felt. Carefully place gem into center of paint and gently press down. Let dry.

4 Use fabric glue to add yellow rickrack around the banner edges. Let the glue dry.

5 Use a small amount of wood glue to attach a wood doll head onto each end of the dowel. Let dry.

6 Paint the dowel and the wood balls green. Let dry.

7 Fold the top of the felt banner around the dowel and glue it to the back side of felt using fabric glue.

8 Cut a 30-inch piece of ribbon. Fold it in half and tie a big bow in the center. Tie a knot in each ribbon end close to the bow. Keeping the bow centered, loop each end of the ribbon onto ends of the dowel.

continued on page 24

BOO BANNER LETTERING PATTERN

1 SQUARE = 1 INCH

Like dew on a real web, these beaded versions glisten in the sunlight. Make them in black or white; then perch the wire web spinners close by.

spiderweb

supplies

Wire cutters
20-gauge white or
   black wire
6-mm black
   faceted beads or
   6-mm pearl beads
Pliers; 24-gauge
   silver wire
Yardstick
Monofilament
   thread

what to do

1 Cut four lengths of 20-gauge wire 2 to 3 feet long for a larger web or 1 to 1½ feet long for a smaller web. Cut a 2½-inch length of wire and wrap it three times around the center of all four wires to secure. Twist the short wire ends together and then trim off any excess.

2 Spread out the wires to become the spokes of the web. Work with one spoke at a time and thread the entire length with beads. Turn over the wire end with pliers. The loop will prevent the beads from falling off. Continue until the remaining spokes are completed.

3 Cut a 2-foot length (reduce the length if making the smaller web) of 24-gauge wire. Twist the end around one of the beaded spokes 1½ inches out from the center of the web. Thread seven to nine beads onto the wire and then wrap it around the next spoke. Continue threading beads and wrapping the wire around each spoke until the web is encircled. Twist the wire end and trim remaining wire.

4 Cut a 3-foot length of 24-gauge wire for the next circle of the web. Work around the web again, increasing the number of beads to fill the space between spokes. Cut a longer wire and increase the number of beads for the third time around the web. Hang the web from thread.

spider

supplies

Wire cutters; ruler
18-gauge yellow
   craft wire; pliers
2 black faceted or
   pearl beads

what to do

1 Cut five 5-inch lengths of wire. Group four of the wires together. Tightly wrap one end of the fifth wire around the center of the group four times. Spiral the end of the fifth wire to make the body.

2 Separate the spider's legs and loop over each end to make its feet. Thread two bead eyes on a 2-inch length of 24-gauge wire.

Position the beads over the top of the wrapped wire body. Bring the wire ends down between the first and second legs on either side. Twist the ends together under the body and then trim away any excess wire.

scaredy-cat plate

Perfect for serving ghoulish Halloween cookies or for displaying on a plate stand, this painted glass plate features a devilish black cat.

CAT FACE PATTERN

supplies

Clear glass dinner plate
Tracing paper
Pencil
Scissors; tape
Glass paints in black, white, red, yellow, and orange
Paintbrush

what to do

1 Wash and dry the plate. Avoid touching the areas to be painted.

2 Trace the cat pattern, *above.* Trim pattern close to design. Tape pattern, right side down, to center of plate front. Turn over to allow painting on back.

3 Using the pattern as a guide, paint the black outlines for the cat. Let dry. Paint the colored areas on the cat. To make gray for the fur, mix white with black. Let dry.

4 To make black dots, dip the eraser of a pencil into paint. Make dots randomly around the cat. Let dry. Paint the orange background. Let dry.

5 Remove the pattern. Use a small, flat paintbrush to make alternating yellow and black checks along the plate rim, leaving a small space between each mark. Let dry. Bake the painted plate in the oven if instructed by the paint manufacturer. Let cool.

Note: Do not soak plate. Wash top gently with warm water and wipe dry.

trick-or-treat tree

Decked out in Halloween colors, this candy tree looks good enough to eat!

supplies
Long sticks
Clear spray
  varnish
Pumpkin
Drill; needle
Dental floss
Candy in
  Halloween colors

Candy worms
Miniature popcorn
  balls wrapped in
  colored
  cellophane and
  tied with
  curling ribbon

what to do
1 Wash the sticks. Let them dry. In a well-ventilated work area, spray the

continued on page 32

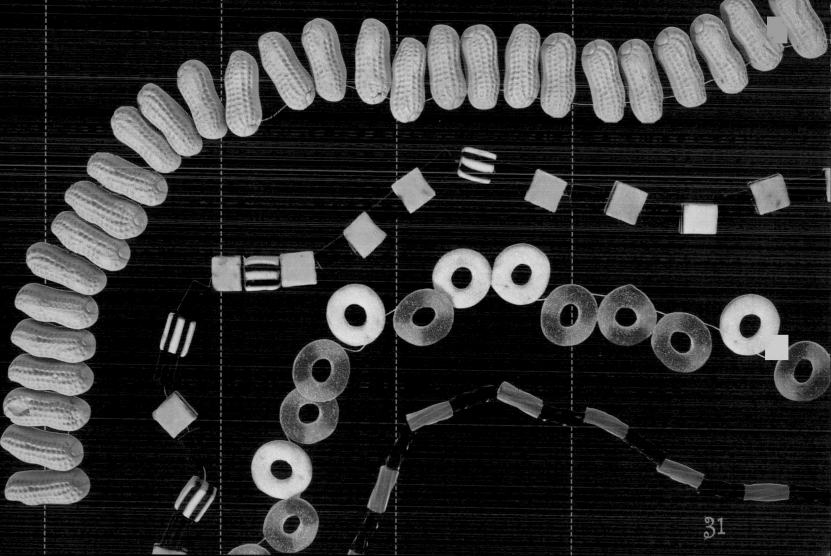

sticks with varnish. Let the varnish dry.

2 Drill small holes in the top of the pumpkin where sticks are desired. Push the sticks in the drilled holes.

3 To make a candy garland, thread a needle with floss. Thread candy on floss as desired. Knot at the ends. Make garlands with a variety of candy shapes as shown on *page 31.*

4 Hang the garlands, worms, and popcorn balls on the tree.

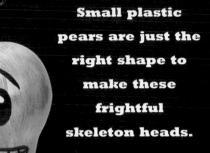

Small plastic pears are just the right shape to make these frightful skeleton heads.

scary skeleton garland

supplies

Small plastic pears on wire stems

Acrylic enamel paints in white and black

Paintbrush

Lime green plastic lacing

Pony beads in black, white, orange, purple, and lime green

what to do

1 Paint the pears with a light coat of white, allowing some of the pear color to show through. Paint the wire stems black. Let the paint dry. Using the patterns, *below,* as guides, paint faces on the pears to resemble skeleton heads. Let the paint dry. Add white accents to the eyes if desired. Let dry.

2 String 5 inches of pony beads on the lacing as desired. Tie the lacing to the wire at the top of the skeleton. Continue stringing on beads and skeleton heads in this manner until the desired length is achieved.

Light the path to your haunted mansion with these clever milk jug luminarias. For little investment, you can make enough characters to line your drive on Halloween night.

eerie luminarias

supplies

Gallon plastic
  jugs rinsed with
  labels removed
Utility knife
Tracing paper
Pencil; scissors
Tape
Paint markers in
  silver, orange,
  green, yellow,
  red, and black
Goo Be Gone
Paper towels and
  cotton swabs
Monster: 2 each
  of bolts, nuts,
  washers, white
  and black
  crafting foam
  scraps, such as
  Fun Foam
Thick white
  crafts glue
Cat: two 12-inch
  lengths of
  20-gauge steel
  wire
Darning needle
  and pliers
Sand and
  candles,
  flashlight, or a
  string of lights

what to do

1 Carefully cut
  the spout and
handle off the jug.
Enlarge and trace
the patterns, *pages
36–37.* Cut out face
patterns and tape
to the inside of
the jugs.

2 Outline the
  skull with
silver; the monster
head with green;
and the cat with
black. To spread
the color over the
face of the jug,
squeeze a few
drops of Goo Be
Gone onto a folded
paper towel and
rub it over the
paint marker.
Continue working
around the edges,
wiping the paint
toward the center
of your design. If
you're working on
the skull, you'll
need to draw an
additional line of
orange around the
skull and then
spread it outward
with the paper
towel and Goo Be
Gone. Let dry.

3 After the paint
  has dried, add
eyes, nose, teeth,
hair, and scar with
the different
colored paint
markers. Remove
any mistakes or
unwanted marks by
squeezing Goo Be
Gone onto the end
of a cotton swab
and then wiping
away the problem
spot (use paper
towel for larger
areas). Once you're
pleased with your
design, outline the
features with the
black paint marker.

4 To insert the
  bolts in the
monster's neck,
prepoke a hole on
each side of his
neck with scissors.
Thread a washer
onto the bolt and
push it through the
hole. Reaching
inside the jug,
screw a nut onto
the end of the bolt.
Use the cat ear,
collar, and bow tie
patterns to cut
pieces from foam.
Slip the collar
under the washers
and glue the bow
tie to the center of
the collar. Glue the
cat ears in place.

5 To thread the
  whiskers onto
the cat, prepoke
two holes on each
side of the nose
with a needle and
poke the wire into
a hole on one side
of the nose and out
the hole on the
other side. Repeat
the process with
the second wire.
Use pliers to make
curls on ends of
the wires.

continued on page 36

6 If using candles to light the luminarias, pour 2 to 3 inches of sand in the bottom of each jug. Place a candle in the center.

Note: Never leave a burning candle unattended.

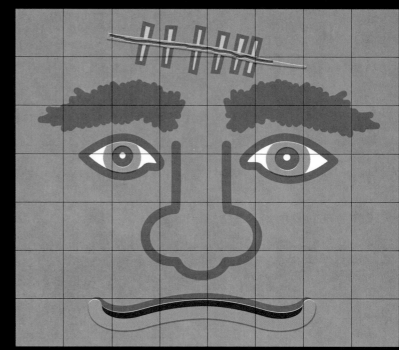

FRANKENSTEIN LUMINARIA   **1 SQUARE = 1 INCH**

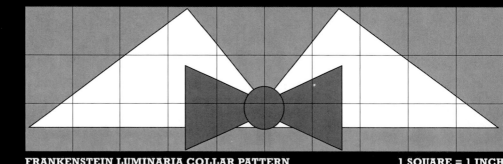

FRANKENSTEIN LUMINARIA COLLAR PATTERN   **1 SQUARE = 1 INCH**

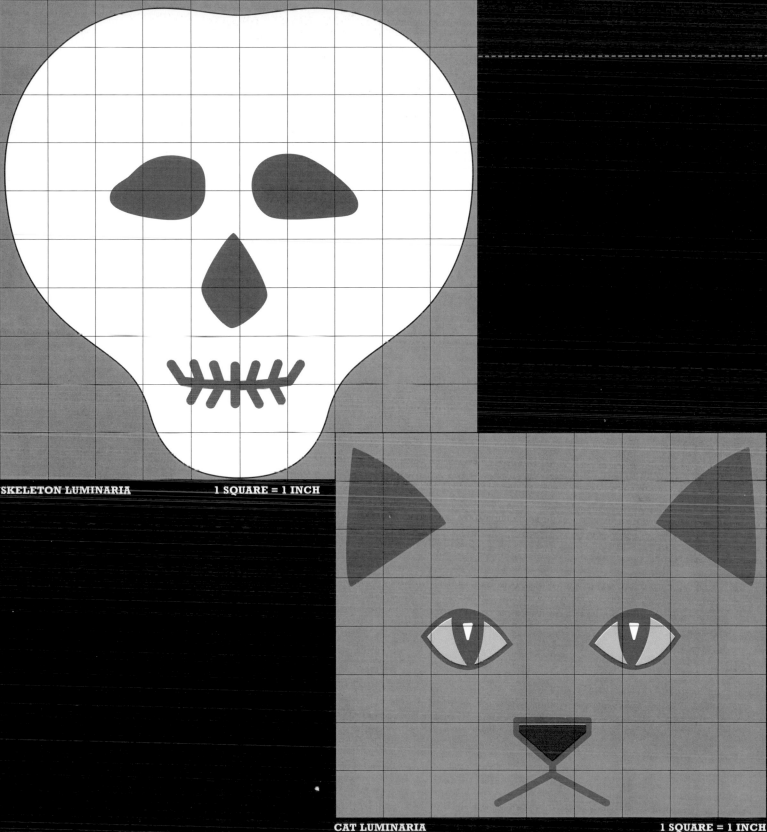

SKELETON LUMINARIA   1 SQUARE = 1 INCH

CAT LUMINARIA   1 SQUARE = 1 INCH

pumpkin wreath

Welcome Halloween visitors with a cheerful wreath of animated pumpkins. Use our wreath for inspiration, but have fun making your own funny faces from lightweight clay. Drape the wreath with artificial spiderwebbing to complete the look.

supplies

- **10-inch wreath form of wire or foam, such as Styrofoam**
- **Wide masking tape**
- **Air-dry clay, such as Crayola Model Magic**
- **Rolling pin**
- **2- to $3\frac{1}{2}$-inch round biscuit or cookie cutters**
- **Sharp knife**
- **Thick white crafts glue; toothpick**
- **Acrylic paint in orange, yellow, black, and green**
- **Paintbrush**
- **Strong adhesive, such as E6000**
- **Black curling ribbon; scissors**
- **Artificial webbing**

what to do

1 Using masking tape, wrap the wreath form until covered. Set aside.

2 To make pumpkins, roll out clay about $\frac{1}{8}$ inch thick. Cut circles with various sizes of the round cutters. Work quickly as the clay dries fast. Keep extra clay tightly wrapped.

3 Distort the circles slightly by pulling into oblong shapes as desired. Use a knife to press curved lines into the pumpkins.

4 Form clay eyes, noses, and mouths. Cut rectangular shapes for stems. Position the pieces on the pumpkins. Use a toothpick and a dab of crafts glue to attach them. Cut simple leaf shapes. Use the knife to draw leaf veins.

5 After the clay is dry, paint the pumpkins orange, the stems green, and the facial features yellow and black. Let dry.

6 Generously apply adhesive to pumpkin backs and leaves. Attach to wreath form using the photo, *opposite*, as a guide. Let dry.

7 To curl pieces of ribbon, hold scissors at an angle against ribbon, pulling ribbon taut against blade. Glue ribbons between the clay pieces. Let dry. Add webbing as desired.

pumpkin patch candle

Pieces of wire appear to lace the miniature pumpkins together as they encircle a towering candle. Dripping with white wax and orange and black glitter, the three-wick candle adds the finishing touch to this clever centerpiece for your Halloween table.

supplies

White wax, candle, or paraffin
Old metal saucepan and tin can
3-wick black candle
Orange and black glitter
Approximately 10 miniature pumpkins; ruler
18-gauge wire
Wire cutters; awl
Soup can; pliers
Small, round tray

what to do

1 To melt wax, break up pieces and place in tin can. Place can in a saucepan filled halfway with water. Heat on stove until melted, never leaving the wax unattended. Pour the wax over top and edges of the black candle. Sprinkle glitter over the wet wax.

2 Cut ten 6-inch-long and ten 3-inch-long pieces of wire. If using more pumpkins, you will need to cut more wires.

3 Bend the long pieces of wire around a soup can to shape into an arch. Use pliers to shape the short pieces of wire into Vs.

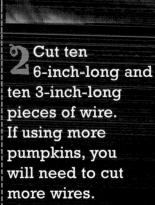

4 With an awl, poke holes into the top of each pumpkin as shown in the photos, *below and opposite.*

5 Arrange the candle and pumpkins on a tray. Insert the wires into the pumpkins as shown.

Note: Never leave a burning candle unattended.

shrieking shakers

They don't really make noise, but you might! Pick a favorite Halloween toy to place inside your one-of-a-kind shaker to make it as scary or as silly as you like. These clever toys make great party favors for special ghouls and boys.

supplies
Small plastic Halloween toys such as spiders, pumpkins, skeletons, mummies, witches, etc.
Pencil
Glass jar and lid
Plastic yogurt or margarine lid
Scissors
Hot-glue gun and glue sticks
Thumbtacks
Glycerin
Glitter, sequins, and confetti
Food coloring in green, yellow, and blue
Paper towel
Feather boa

what to do

1 Select a toy to place inside the jar. Trace the top of the jar lid onto a plastic lid and cut out the circle. Anchor the base of the toy to the plastic circle by first hot-gluing it and pushing thumbtacks up through the underside of the circle and into the base of the toy. Note that the pumpkin ball, *opposite,* is not anchored to the jar. Place the plastic lid inside the jar lid.

2 Fill the jar halfway with water and the remainder with glycerin, being sure to allow enough space to accommodate the toy. Sprinkle glitter, sequins, and confetti in any combination into the filled jar. If you'd like to color the jar green, place a half drop each of green and yellow food coloring into the water-glycerin mix. If you'd like to make the water blue, simply add a half drop of blue into the mix.

3 Screw the jar lid tightly in place. Invert it onto a paper towel to test for leaks. Hot-glue around the edge of the lid and wrap the feather boa around the glue. Trim away excess. Glue a plastic spider to the top of the jar if desired.

carve and

paint them

pumpkins—pumpkins—pumpkins!

party pumpkins

Whether resting on the front stoop or atop your party table, these pumpkins will delight one and all. Within minutes you can make either of these unusual pumpkins.

color-blast pumpkin

supplies
Pumpkin
Quilting pins with colored heads
Crafting foam shapes
Gold flathead straight pins

what to do
1 Add foam shapes to the pumpkin, securing each foam piece with a quilting pin in its center.

2 Between foam shapes, add three gold pins. Poke the pins into the pumpkin, making triangular shapes. Continue until the pumpkin is covered.

paint-drip pumpkin

supplies
Pumpkin
Gold spray paint
Lime green glass spray paint
White acrylic paint
Paintbrush
White glitter paint

what to do
1 Lightly spray the top portion of the pumpkin with gold spray paint. Let dry.

2 Lightly spray a lime green glass paint over the gold area. Let dry.

3 Paint small drips and dots with white acrylic paint. Let dry. Paint over white acrylic paint with white glitter paint. Let dry.

joyful pumpkins

The stacked-up pumpkin pals, *opposite*, will make you giggle right along with them, while purple, glittery polka dots add razzle-dazzle to the striking pumpkin, *below*.

stacked-up pumpkins

supplies
Large, medium, and small pumpkins
Spoon
Carving knife
Beaded garland
Candles
Long-handled matches

what to do
1 Cut the top of each pumpkin and scoop out the insides. Stack the pumpkins in descending order by size. Trim the top holes, if necessary, so they sit firmly together. Dismantle the trio.

2 Carve desired faces in the pumpkins. Place a candle in each pumpkin. Carefully restack the pumpkins.

3 Wrap the pumpkin trio with a long length of beaded garland as shown, *opposite*.

4 Light the candles through the openings. Place the lid on the top pumpkin.

Note: For safety, do not leave burning candles unattended.

polka-dot pumpkin

supplies
Pumpkin
Gold spray paint
Purple glitter paint
Paintbrush

what to do
1 Lightly spray the top portion of the pumpkin with gold spray paint. Let dry.

2 Using the photo, *left,* as a guide, paint on polka dots with purple glitter paint. Let dry.

hydrangea pumpkin

A cloud of hydrangea makes a beautiful presentation for the Halloween table when tucked into the top of a natural green and orange pumpkin.

supplies

Medium or large pumpkin
Sharp knife
Spoon
Scissors
Fresh-cut or artificial hydrangea
Plastic liner, optional

what to do

1 Cut a circle around the pumpkin stem. Scoop out the pumpkin using a spoon.

2 Use scissors to cut the hydrangea stems to an appropriate length when placed inside the pumpkin. If using fresh-cut flowers, place a plastic liner in the pumpkin before arranging the flowers.

grommet and eyelet gourds

Sewing notions take on a funky new look when adorning autumn gourds.

Press five more grommets 1 inch above the first row, centering them between the grommets in the first row. Wind orange floss around the grommets as shown, *left*.

2 For the green gourd, press ten gold eyelets equally spaced around the center of the gourd. Press ten more eyelets ¾ inch above the first row, centering them between the eyelets in the first row. Wind purple floss around the eyelets.

3 For the orange gourd, randomly press silver, white, copper, and black eyelets into the gourd. Cut a 10-inch piece of wire. Wrap the center of the wire around the stem. Coil the ends.

supplies
Gourds
Gold grommets
Eyelets in gold, silver, black, copper, and white

Embroidery floss in orange and purple
Black craft wire
Wire cutters

what to do
1 For the tall gourd, press five grommets equally spaced around the center of the gourd.

swirl-top pumpkin

Both elegant and easy, this glistening pumpkin can be enjoyed all autumn long. Metallic red spray paint highlights the pumpkin top, acting as a backdrop for golden swirls of glitter paint to dance around the stem.

supplies
Pumpkin
Newspapers
Metallic red
  spray paint
Gold glitter fabric
  paint pen

what to do

1 Wash the pumpkin to remove any surface dirt. Let the pumpkin dry.

2 In a well-ventilated work area, cover the work surface with newspapers. Place the pumpkin in the center of the newspapers.

3 Lightly spray the top of the pumpkin with metallic red spray paint. Let the paint dry.

4 Use a gold glitter paint pen to draw swirls or other desired designs over the painted area of the pumpkin. Add touches of paint pen to the stem. Let the paint dry.

For a fanciful
presentation,
dress up bright
orange pumpkins
in glistening
metallic beads,
gold foil leafing,
stars, and ribbon.
They're sure to
set a festive
mood all
autumn long.

elegant pumpkins

beaded pumpkins

supplies
Large and small
  pumpkins
Beaded garland
Straight pins
Wide wire-edged
  ribbon
Star sequins
Quilting pins
Beading wire
Beads

what to do
1 For the large
  pumpkin, attach
one end of the
garland at the stem
base. Pin in place.
Loop the garland
down halfway,
bring back up to
the stem, and pin.
Continue making
loops around the
entire pumpkin top.
Tie a generous
ribbon bow around
the stem.
2 For the small
  pumpkin, attach
star sequins with
quilting pins.
Thread beads on
three lengths of
wire. Add a star
sequin and bead to
one end of each
wire. Thread wire
back through star
and beads to
secure. Poke wires
at the opposite
ends next to the
stem. Secure a
bead and star on
the end of a piece
of wire. Poke into
stem and shape
as desired.

gilded pumpkins

supplies
Dry, firm
  pumpkins
Adhesive for gold
  leafing
Paintbrush
Gold foil leafing

what to do
1 Paint the
  pumpkin with a
coat of adhesive for
use with gold foil.
Paint the top first.
When tacky, turn
over the pumpkin
and paint the
bottom. Let the
adhesive dry
to a tacky, but
not wet, stage.
2 Gently apply
  gold foil leaf in
small pieces to the
tacky surface,
smoothing out the
wrinkles. Repeat
until the pumpkin is
completely covered.

painted pumpkins

supplies
**Dry, firm, small
pumpkins
Acrylic paints in
black, white, red,
green, purple,
aqua, or other
desired colors
Paintbrush**

what to do
1 Decide what
design to paint
on the pumpkin.
Paint a design, such
as stars, zigzags,
diamond shapes,
stripes, or dots.

2 Paint the
background
areas and let dry.
To make dots, dip
the eraser of
a pencil or the
handle of a
paintbrush into
paint and dot onto
the surface. Make
double dots by
painting smaller
dots over larger
ones, letting dry
between coats.
Use a fine liner
brush to make
stripes and
outlines. Let the
paint dry.

**These miniature
works of art can
incorporate your
favorite motifs and
colors. Decorate
them with acrylic
paint to add
creative hints of
autumn all around
the house.**

wacky wired gourds

Available in a rainbow of metallic colors, shiny craft wire adds contemporary pizzazz to this pair of gourds.

supplies
Wire cutters
Ruler
Fine colored metallic wire (available at crafts and art stores)
Ice pick
Miniature gourds

what to do

1 For the striped coil pumpkin, cut 8-inch lengths of wire. Wrap each length tightly around the ice pick, leaving 1 inch straight on each end. Make six to nine coils. To place on pumpkin, first use the ice pick to poke holes around the stem and at the bottom of the pumpkin, following the seams of the pumpkin. Poke a wire end in each hole to secure.

2 For the swirl pumpkin, cut a 14-inch length of wire. Fold the wire in half. Form each end into a swirl. Shape small loops between the swirls. Use an ice pick to poke a hole in the top of the pumpkin near the stem. Push the center fold of the wire into the hole.

peekaboo pumpkin

Fun for a Halloween party or any autumn get-together, these silly characters are right at home in their stout pumpkin birdhouse.

supplies

Pumpkin
Spoon
Knife or drill with 1¼-inch bit
Acrylic paints in black, lavender, blue, green, pink, yellow, or other desired colors
Paintbrush
Five 1¼-inch wood doll heads
Thick white crafts glue
¼-inch plastic wiggly eyes
Air-dry clay, such as Crayola Model Magic
Scissors
Thick lead-free solder wire or armature wire
Ruler
Wire cutters
Large marking pen or 1-inch dowel

what to do

1 Cut a small hole in the bottom of pumpkin. Remove the bottom piece of pumpkin shell. Clean out the inside of the pumpkin using a spoon. Cut or drill five 1¼-inch holes randomly around the pumpkin.

2 To make the bird heads, paint each wood doll head with the desired color and let dry. Glue on two wiggly eyes as shown, *left.*

3 Shape beaks from small pieces of clay. Use pieces about the size of a grape. Shape the clay into cones and slice narrow end with scissors, beginning at the tips. Do not slice all the way across. Spread the clay apart to form open beaks. Let the clay dry. Paint the beaks yellow or black. Let the paint dry. Glue the beaks onto the bird heads below the eyes. Let the glue dry.

4 Cut five wire pieces 4 to 8 inches long. To form into a coil, wrap each around a large marking pen or 1-inch dowel. Insert one end of the wire into the hole in the back of the wood bird head, widening the hole with a pencil if needed. Glue the wire in place. Insert the other end of the wire into the pumpkin inside each hole.

mini pumpkin topiary

Welcome autumn and Halloween visitors with an arrangement that takes advantage of the season's harvest. Miniature gourds are readily available at farmer's markets and grocery stores in the fall.

supplies

3 miniature pumpkins in graduated sizes
Wire coat hanger
Wire cutters
Hot-glue gun and glue sticks
Small terra-cotta pot
Crafts foam
U-pins
Silk or fresh autumn leaves
Green acrylic paint
Sea sponge or cellulose sponge
Bittersweet; raffia

what to do

1. Cut two 2-inch pieces of wire from a coat hanger as shown in Photo 1, *right*.
2. Insert one end of a piece of wire into or beside the stem of the bottom pumpkin. Place a drop of glue where the wire enters the pumpkin as shown in Photo 2.
3. Insert the other end of the wire into the bottom of the middle pumpkin (Photo 3).
4. Attach the top pumpkin to the middle pumpkin in the same manner.
5. Using the sea sponge, pat green paint onto the terra-cotta pot, allowing the clay color to show through. If desired, use a cellulose sponge by tearing away pieces from the surface to roughen it.
6. Fill the pot almost to the top with crafts foam. Pin a collar of leaves to the foam with U-pins. Insert a short piece of coat hanger wire into the bottom pumpkin, then push the other end into the crafts foam. Tie raffia around the rim of the pot, and glue sprigs of bittersweet to the raffia.

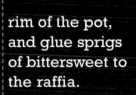

You'll love pulling out this striking stand from your bag of tricks each Halloween. Then decorate a pumpkin to set on top for a spirited duo.

pretty pumpkin & stand

supplies

- Two 9½-inch wood plates
- Pencil; ruler
- Drill; ⅛- and ¹⁄₁₆-inch drill bits
- 7-inch stool leg
- Two 1-inch wood screws
- Screwdriver
- Wood glue
- Black spray paint
- Decoupage medium
- Paintbrush
- Glitter in purple, orange, lime green, and black
- Silver glitter glue
- 16 gems, 8 gold and 8 purple
- Copper wire
- Wire cutters
- Metallic purple beads
- Needlenose pliers
- Pumpkin

what to do

1 To make the stand, mark the center of each wood plate. Using a ⅛-inch bit, drill a hole in the center of each plate. Using wood screws, attach the plates to the stool leg, with the plate bottoms facing the leg ends. Add wood glue to the ends of the stool leg before tightening the screws. Let dry.

2 In a well-ventilated work area, spray-paint the stand black. Let dry.

3 On the stand top, measure and mark 16 equally spaced dots ¼ inch in from the edge. Using a ¹⁄₁₆-inch bit, drill a hole at each dot.

4 On the rim of the top plate, brush on decoupage medium. While wet, sprinkle with purple glitter. Add different colors of glitter to the stool leg, working on one section at a time. To add stripes to the base plate, paint wide stripes approximately 1 inch apart using decoupage medium. Sprinkle with purple glitter. Add narrow green glitter stripes between the purple stripes. Let dry.

5 Between each drilled hole, add a pea-size dot of glitter glue. Place a gem on each dot of glue, alternating gold and purple. Let dry.

6 Cut sixteen 6-inch-long pieces of wire. Using needlenose pliers, coil one end of each wire, leaving 1 inch straight. Slip a bead on the straight ends. Poke the wires up through the holes in the top plate. Use the pliers to make small loops at the ends of the wires to secure.

7 To trim the pumpkin, use a pencil to draw a checkerboard on the pumpkin. Using decoupage medium, paint two or three squares and then sprinkle with black glitter. Continue until the design is complete. Add purple glitter triangles, squares,

and rectangles in between the black areas. Paint decoupage medium on the stem and sprinkle with green glitter. Let dry.

Glowing candles are a must
at Halloween, and
a glowing candelabra or
pumpkin trio are just right for
the eerie occasion.

glowing pumpkins

pumpkin candelabra

supplies

Small pumpkins, one for each holder of the candelabra; knife
Drill and large bit
Pony beads
Sequins
Quilting pins
Short taper candles
Iron candelabra
Ribbon

what to do

1 Wash and dry the pumpkins. Cut off the stems. Drill holes large enough to hold a candle in each pumpkin top.

2 Use pins to attach beads and sequins randomly to the pumpkins.

3 Place pumpkins on holders of candelabra. Insert a candle in each top. Tie a ribbon bow around the center of the candelabra. Light the candles.

jesting jack-o'-lanterns

supplies

3 pumpkins approximately the same size
Carving knife
Spoon; candles

what to do

1 Decide how you want the trio arranged. Trim off one side of each outer pumpkin so they can sit close together. Cut the bottom off the center pumpkin.

2 Scoop out the insides of the pumpkins. Carve desired faces on the pumpkins.

3 Place candles in each of the pumpkins. Light the candles.

Note: Do not leave burning candles unattended.

sequin-striped pumpkin

As elegant as a
dancer's dress,
this pumpkin
dons stripes of
sequins in silver
and black.

supplies
Tape measure
Pumpkin
Sequins on a
  string in silver
  and black
Scissors
Straight pins with
  black heads
Silver cord

what to do
1 Measure the
pumpkin from
the stem to the
bottom center. Use
this measurement
to cut lengths from
sequin strings.

2 Using the
pumpkin seams
as guides, pin the
sequins vertically
on the pumpkin,
alternating colors.

3 Wrap the stem
with silver cord.
Use pins to secure
the ends.

You don't need to be an artist to produce masterpieces on gourd canvases.

autumn-touched gourds

supplies
Small, dried ornamental gourds
Plastic scraper
Sharp knife; pencil
Assorted leaves
Wood-burning tool with fine tip
Watercolor markers in purple, pink, red, green, orange, and yellow
Medium-size soft paintbrush
Clear varnish

what to do

1 Choose gourds with a fairly smooth, clean surface. They should be dry, hard, and hollow-sounding. Soak and clean the gourds with warm soapy water, using a plastic scraper. Scrape off any rough areas with a sharp knife. Wipe dry.

2 Using a pencil, trace around leaves on gourd.

3 Using a wood-burning tool with a very fine tip, outline the leaf shapes and draw in veins. Using the photo, *above,* as inspiration, color the outlined areas with watercolor markers, overlapping colors slightly. To create a shaded look, color purple next to pink or red and green next to orange or yellow.

4 Dip a medium-size soft paintbrush in water and wipe off the excess. Brush onto the areas covered with markers to blend colors. Let dry.

5 Paint a coat of clear varnish over the gourd, blending the colors once again. Do not overbrush or the colors will become muddy and run.

Carved, painted, or wrapped in sequins, these star-embellished pumpkins are stunning alone or in a grouping.

starstruck pumpkins

supplies

Pumpkins of all sizes
Fabric paint pen in desired color
Paring knife
Spoon
Votive candle
Star sequins
Pearl-head quilting pins
Small star cookie cutter

what to do

1. To make the paint-pen pumpkin, draw stars in desired colors all over the pumpkin. Let the paint dry.

2. To make the candleholder pumpkin, use a paring knife to cut a round hole large enough to hold a votive candle. Use a spoon to scoop out enough space to insert candle. Decorate around the hole with paint pen as desired. Place a votive candle into the hole.

3. To make the sequined pumpkin, attach star sequins using quilting pins.

4. To make the cookie-cutter pumpkin, press the star cookie cutter into the surface of the pumpkin and remove the skin of the star shape using a paring knife. Repeat as desired.

Note: Never leave a burning candle unattended.

These playful pranksters will have you cackling with delight. Made from small gourds, the fiendish duo is trimmed with crafting foam accents.

gourd ghouls

supplies

- Small pear-shape gourds
- White spray-paint primer
- Paper punch
- Crafting foam in white, black, orange, and yellow; scissors
- White quilting or map pins
- Fine-line black permanent marking pen
- Tracing paper
- Pencil
- Thick white crafts glue; clothespin
- Acrylic paints in black and white
- Paintbrush
- Colored wire in orange and purple

what to do

1 In a well-ventilated work area, spray-paint the gourds white. Let dry.

2 To make eyes, punch out black circles from crafting foam. Using the photo, *opposite,* for placement, attach the black circles to the gourds using white quilting or map pins. Use a black marking pen to draw mouths and make a dot for each nose.

3 Trace the patterns, *right.* Cut out. Trace around the patterns on crafting foam. Cut out the shapes. Glue the details on the pumpkin shape. Let dry. To make eyes on the bat, dip the handle of a paintbrush into white paint and dot onto the foam. When dry, make a tiny black dot in the center of each eye using a black marking pen.

4 To make wire coil, wrap the entire orange wire around a pencil and remove. For the purple wire, wrap half of the wire.

Shape the remaining end into a zigzag, making a spiral at the end. Glue the jack-o'-lantern to the top of the purple coil. Glue the bat to the top of the orange coil. Let dry.

5 Pin the arms into place. For the tall gourd, place the orange coiled wire into position. Glue the right foam hand over the wire, securing with a clothespin until dry.

6 Slip hat brim over the top of the short gourd. Paint the gourd black above the brim. Let dry. Slip the purple wire into place.

7 If the gourds roll, poke pins into the bottoms to steady them.

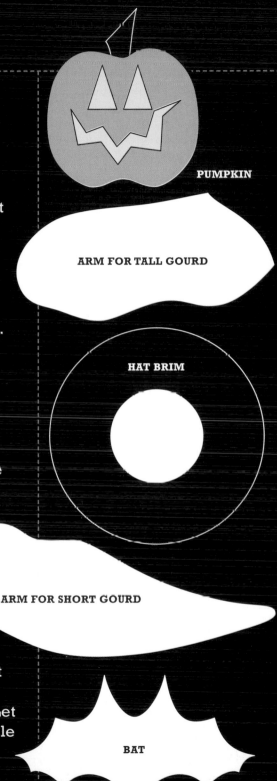

PUMPKIN

ARM FOR TALL GOURD

HAT BRIM

ARM FOR SHORT GOURD

BAT

sparkling pumpkins

supplies
**Pumpkin with
  long stem
Paintbrush
White glue
Glitter in purple,
  lime green, or
  other desired
  color**

**Silver curling
  ribbon
Scissors**

what to do

1 Choose a pumpkin with a long stem. Wash and dry the pumpkin.

2 Use a paintbrush to apply glue to the stem. While the glue is wet, sprinkle with glitter. Let dry.

3 Cut 2-foot lengths of ribbon. To curl pieces of ribbon, hold scissors at an angle against ribbon, pulling ribbon taut against blade. Place one or two ribbons around the stem.

Pumpkins of any size become glamorous instantly with glittery stems draped with curling ribbon.

darling daisy pumpkin

Abloom with autumn flowers, this no-carve pumpkin can be put together at the last minute.

supplies
Pumpkin
Knife; spoon
Drill and ¼-inch bit
Scissors
Daisies

what to do
1 Cut the top off the pumpkin. Scoop out. Using a drill, make holes randomly around the pumpkin.

2 Cut stems of daisies to appropriate length for the pumpkin. Push stems through the holes, arranging as desired.

charming pumpkin box

When the light falls upon this paper pumpkin, the glitter will sparkle with vibrant color. Use it to hold Halloween candy or other treasures for your favorite kids in costume.

supplies

Pencil
Ruler
Hollow brown paper pumpkin (available in crafts stores)
Sharp utility or crafts knife
Acrylic paints in orange, green, and white
Paintbrush
Awl
White glue
Glitter in orange and green
Wire
Wire cutters
Pliers

what to do

1 Draw a horizontal line around the paper pumpkin to indicate where to cut it in half. Cut along the line with a sharp utility or crafts knife.

2 Paint the outside of the pumpkin orange. Paint the inside green. Add white highlights if desired. Let the paint dry.

3 Use an awl to pierce holes through the stem and on each side of the bottom piece as shown, *opposite,* to insert wire.

4 Coat the outside of the pumpkin and stem with white glue. Sprinkle orange and green glitters onto the wet glue. Let the glue dry.

5 Cut a piece of wire approximately 20 inches long. Insert the wire into the hole in the pumpkin stem. Wrap the wire ends around a pencil three or four times to make a coil. Insert the wire ends into the holes in the bottom piece. To secure, pinch the ends up with pliers. Adjust the lid as desired.

treat them

right

goodies for the ghostly group

halloween brews

Whether you're chilled to the bone or in need of a cool potion, try one of these delicious concoctions. The Hot Golden Cider, *top left,* has a caramel-flavored candy stirring stick. You can cool off with a cup of red Transylvania Punch that tastes of cherry and lemon-lime. The last of our cold brews, Orange Cream Punch, includes sherbet to make it a frosty delight. Our other warmer-upper, Haunting Hot Chocolate, has a marshmallow ghost garnish. The recipes are on pages 82–83.

81

halloween brews continued

ORANGE CREAM PUNCH

hot golden cider

supplies

6 cups apple
  cider
2 12½-ounce cans
  apricot nectar
2 tablespoons
  packed brown
  sugar
100 percent
  cotton
  cheesecloth
Scissors
String
6-inch-long
  cinnamon sticks
½ teaspoon
  whole cloves
Caramel-flavored
  candy stick,
  optional

what to do

1 In a large
saucepan
combine apple
cider, apricot
nectar, and brown
sugar. Cut a double
thickness of
100 percent cotton
cheesecloth into an
8-inch square.
Combine cinnamon
and cloves in
cheesecloth. Bring
up corners of
cheesecloth and tie
with cotton string.
Add to saucepan.
Bring mixture to
boiling; reduce
heat. Simmer,
covered, for
10 minutes.

2 Remove and
discard spices.
Serve warm.
Garnish with
caramel-flavored
candy stick, if
desired. Makes
twelve 6-ounce
servings.

orange cream punch

supplies

1 14-ounce can
  sweetened
  condensed milk
1 12-ounce can
  frozen orange
  juice
  concentrate,
  thawed
Orange food
  coloring
2 1-liter bottles
  club soda or
  ginger ale,
  chilled
Orange sherbet

what to do

1 In a punch
bowl combine
sweetened
condensed milk
and orange juice
concentrate. Tint
with orange food
coloring, if desired.
Add club soda.

2 Top with
scoops of
orange sherbet.
Serve immediately.
Makes thirty-two
6-ounce servings.

haunting hot chocolate

supplies

1 medium orange
3 cups whole milk
2/3 cup
  vanilla-flavored
  baking pieces or
  vanilla-flavored
  candy coating
1/8 teaspoon
  ground nutmeg
1 teaspoon
  vanilla
Whipped cream,
  optional
Ground nutmeg,
  optional
Purchased
  marshmallow
  ghosts

what to do

1 Remove peel
of orange with
vegetable peeler;
set aside.

2 In a medium
saucepan
combine 1/4 cup
of the milk,
vanilla-flavored
baking pieces,
orange peel, and
nutmeg; whisk over
low heat until
baking pieces are
melted. Remove
orange peel. Whisk
in remaining milk
and heat through.
Remove from heat.
Stir in vanilla.

3 Serve warm in
mugs. Add a
marshmallow
ghost, dollop with
whipped cream,
and sprinkle with
nutmeg, if desired.
Makes five
6-ounce servings.

transylvania punch

supplies

2 cups water
1 3-ounce
  package cherry-
  flavored gelatin
4 12-ounce cans
  lemon-lime or
  ginger ale
  carbonated
  beverage,
  chilled

what to do

1 In a medium
saucepan bring
2 cups water to
boiling. Transfer to
a bowl. Add gelatin
and stir until
gelatin is dissolved.
Cover and chill 4
hours or overnight.

2 To serve, pour
about 1/2 cup of
ginger ale into a
glass. Spoon in an
equal amount of
the chilled gelatin.
(Gelatin should
float atop ginger
ale.) If desired, stir
together just
before drinking.
Makes six 6-ounce
servings.

HAUNTING HOT
CHOCOLATE

Purchased cookie dough is the key to creating these puzzling Halloween sweets.

puzzle cookies

supplies

¼ **cup all-purpose flour**

1 **18-ounce roll refrigerated sugar cookie dough**

1 **recipe Egg Yolk Paint**

what to do

1 In a medium bowl knead flour into sugar cookie dough. Divide dough into 6 portions. On an ungreased cookie sheet, pat each portion into a 5-inch square. Press a well-floured 3- to 4-inch Halloween cookie cutter into the center of the square (use smaller cutters, if desired). Carefully remove cookie cutter without removing dough. Using a table knife, cut outside portion of square into large puzzle pieces.

2 Brush dough puzzle pieces with different colors of Egg Yolk Paint.

3 Bake in a 350° oven for 7 to 8 minutes or until bottoms of cookies just start to brown and centers are set. While still warm, carefully recut pieces with the cookie cutter and knife. Trim edges as needed. Transfer cookies to a wire rack; cool completely. Makes 6 puzzle cookies.

Egg Yolk Paint: In a small mixing bowl beat 2 egg yolks and 2 teaspoons water. Divide mixture among 3 to 4 small bowls. In each bowl, add 2 to 3 drops of liquid food coloring or desired amount of paste food coloring in desired color; mix well. Apply with small, clean paintbrush. If mixture thickens while standing, stir in water, one drop at a time.

Wrap the remaining solder length around the cup. Make a loop in the solder end around the bottom tip of the cup.

5 For the message cup, use a paper punch to make holes on opposite sides of the rim on a black cup. Secure an eyelet in each hole. Snip off the bottom tip of the cup. Group together three 10-inch lengths of orange ribbon. Knot them together in the center. From the inside of the cup, poke the ends of the ribbons through the hole in the tip. Using a silver marking pen, write Halloween messages around the cup, such as trick-or-treat, boo, or Happy Halloween. Add

stars near the tip of the cup. To add orange dots, dip the handle of a paintbrush into orange paint and dot onto the surface. Make dots in groups of three, adding between silver markings. Let dry. Cut a 12-inch length of ribbon. Thread the ribbon through the eyelets to make a handle. Knot the ends.

chocolate peanut popcorn

supplies

10 cups popped popcorn
Nonstick cooking spray
1 cup honey-roasted peanuts
¼ cup butter
⅔ cup light-colored corn syrup
1 4-serving-size

package instant chocolate pudding mix
2 teaspoons vanilla

what to do

1 Discard unpopped kernels. Spray a 17×12×2-inch roasting pan with cooking spray. Place the popcorn and peanuts in the pan. Keep warm in 300° oven while making coating.

2 In a medium saucepan melt butter. Remove from heat. Stir in corn syrup, pudding mix, and vanilla. Pour syrup mixture over popcorn. With a large spoon, gently toss the popcorn with the syrup mixture to coat.

3 Bake uncovered, in 300° oven for 15 minutes, stirring once halfway

through cooking time. Remove from oven. Turn mixture onto a large piece of foil. Cool completely. When cool, break into pieces. Store tightly covered in a cool, dry place up to 1 week. Makes about 13 cups.

fruity popcorn

supplies

10 cups popped popcorn
Nonstick cooking spray
1 cup butter
¾ cup sugar
1 3-ounce package orange- or lime-flavored gelatin
3 tablespoons water
1 tablespoon light-colored corn syrup

what to do

1 Discard unpopped

kernels. Spray a 17×12×2-inch roasting pan with cooking spray. Place the popcorn in the pan. Keep warm in 300° oven while making coating.

2 Butter the bottom and sides of a 2-quart saucepan. In the pan combine butter, sugar, gelatin, water, and corn syrup. Cook mixture over medium heat until boiling, stirring constantly. Clip a candy thermometer to the side of the pan. Continue cooking over medium heat, stirring constantly, until the thermometer registers 255° (hard-ball stage), about 10 minutes.

3 Remove saucepan from heat. Pour mixture over popcorn in roasting pan; stir gently to coat. Bake in 300° oven for 5 minutes. Stir mixture. Bake 5 minutes more. Turn mixture onto a large piece of foil; cool. When cool, break into pieces. Store tightly covered in a cool, dry place up to 3 days. Makes about 13 cups.

italian-seasoned popcorn

supplies

3 tablespoons butter
2 tablespoons grated Parmesan cheese
1 teaspoon dried Italian seasoning, crushed
1 teaspoon dried parsley flakes, crushed
½ teaspoon garlic salt
8 cups popped popcorn

what to do

1 Melt the butter in a small saucepan over low heat. Stir in the cheese, Italian seasoning, parsley, and garlic salt.

2 Place the popcorn in a very large mixing bowl. Drizzle the butter mixture over the popcorn; toss gently to coat. Makes about 8 cups.

spicy popcorn

supplies

¼ cup butter
½ teaspoon curry powder
½ teaspoon ground ginger
½ teaspoon chili powder
¼ teaspoon salt
½ teaspoon ground allspice
8 cups popped popcorn
1 cup peanuts
½ cup raisins

what to do

1 Cook the butter in a small saucepan over medium heat until melted and just bubbly. Add curry powder, ginger, chili powder, salt, and allspice. Cook and stir 1 minute more.

2 Combine popcorn, peanuts, and raisins in a large mixing bowl. Drizzle butter mixture over popcorn mixture; toss gently to coat. Makes about 10 cups.

An all-time kids' favorite, these adorable chain rattlers have a cereal and marshmallow base and are coated with vanilla-flavored candy. Have fun making different shapes of ghosts and experiment with different candy bits to create a variety of ghastly, ghostly expressions.

supplies

1 10-ounce bag of marshmallows
¼ cup margarine or butter
6 cups crisp rice cereal
12 ounces vanilla-flavored candy coating, melted
Black licorice candy
Chocolate sprinkles
Miniature semisweet chocolate pieces

what to do

1 In a large pot combine marshmallows and margarine. Cook and stir over medium-low heat until mixture is melted. Gradually stir in cereal until well combined.

2 Use ½ to 1 cup of the cereal mixture per ghost to form into ghost shapes. Set aside to cool completely.

3 Dip each ghost shape into melted candy coating. Use pieces of licorice, chocolate sprinkles, and/or chocolate pieces for the eyes, nose, eyebrows, and mouth. Makes 9 to 12 ghosts.

Don't get spooked, this imaginative forest is completely edible.

supplies

3 stalks of broccoli
3 medium beets
Wood toothpicks
3 hard-boiled eggs
Assorted
  vegetables such
  as cherry
  tomatoes, pea
  pods, kohlrabies,
  radishes, sweet
  red peppers,
  sweet yellow
  peppers, and
  shredded carrot
Ripe olives,
  pimiento-stuffed
  olives, and/or
  tiny sweet pickles
1 ounce spaghetti,
  cooked and
  drained
Liquid green food
  coloring

what to do

1 To make a haunted forest, first create trees. Cut bottoms from stalks of broccoli to make 6-inch broccoli trees. Slice beets about ½ to ¾ inch thick to make a base for broccoli trees. Break wood toothpicks in half. Insert three to four toothpick pieces into bottom of each broccoli stalk and then insert into a beet slice. Stand broccoli upright. Cover to keep moist.

2 To make egg ghosts, use a small knife or ½-inch aspic cutters to hollow out eyes and mouths to form a face. Cut small pieces of ripe olive to press into hollowed-out areas for eyes or mouth, if desired. Cover to keep moist.

3 Using your imagination, create creepy creatures with tomatoes, sweet peppers, pickles, olives, and radishes.

4 Place broccoli trees on serving platter. Cover surface of platter with shredded carrot. Hide egg ghosts in forest along with creepy creatures. Scatter piles of vegetables such as pea pods, beet slices, kohlrabi slices, olives, pickles, and/or any other desired vegetables. Add strips of red pepper to the broccoli branches.

5 To make moss, add a few drops of green food coloring to a small amount of water in a medium bowl. Add cooked spaghetti and let stand about 5 minutes. Drain and place over broccoli trees. Keep platter covered until serving time. If necessary, spritz platter with water to keep it moist.

gumdrop pumpkins

Cut, press, cut, press, and you'll have these darling little pumpkins to help you celebrate at trick-or-treating time. Use them as party favors by placing several gumdrop goodies in a small crate, papier-mâché box, or basket lined with crimped shredded paper. Tuck in a plastic spider ring as the frightful finishing touch.

supplies

Orange slice-shaped jelly candies

Small green gumdrops

what to do

1 To make pumpkins, trim the edges of two orange jelly candies to create straight sides. Push the two sticky sides together, forming a pumpkin shape.

2 Cut a small piece from the bottom of a small green gumdrop. Press into the top of candy pumpkin.

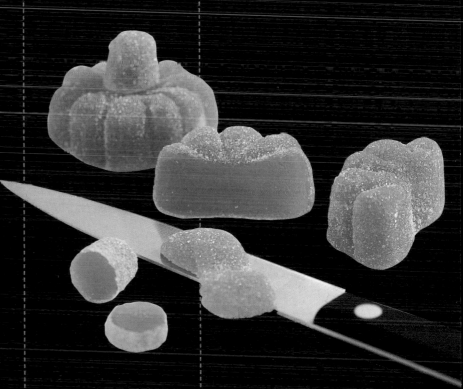

dress them

up

spook-tacular costumes galore

magic tree costume

supplies

- 1 yard of textured fur or bark patterned fleece
- Scissors; 1 yard of quilted backing
- Pins; thread
- 4 feet of ribbon
- Hook and loop fastener
- 1 sheet of brown crafting foam, such as Fun Foam
- Feathered monarch butterflies
- 4 artificial autumn foliage bushes
- Straw hat; moss
- 2 artificial bird's nests, birds, and 4 bird eggs
- Hot-glue gun and glue sticks

what to do

1 To make the tree trunk vest, fold the fabric in half. Lay your child's T-shirt over the folded fabric to serve as a pattern. Cut the fabric 1½ inches from the side and shoulder seams of the T-shirt. The bottom front is cut shorter than the back, which is elongated. Make a V neckline by cutting triangular shapes from neck. Cut two quilted backing pieces: one to match the tree front and one to match the back. Place the right side of the quilted backing over the right side of its matching fur front or back and pin together. Sew around the edge of each set, leaving a 12-inch opening along the side seam. Trim away any excess fabric and turn both vest pieces right side out. Lay the finished front over the finished back, matching right sides together. Pin

As glorious as those from Mother Nature, this realistic tree exhibits barklike fleece, artificial foliage, nests, and butterflies.

the side seams together and then stitch through the four layers of fabric. Sew one end of a 12-inch length of ribbon to each shoulder. The ribbons are tied together over the shoulder after the vest is pulled over the child's head. Hot-glue small strips of brown crafting foam and feathered butterflies to the finished trunk and glue small sections of foliage around the vest neck.

2 To make the wristbands, cut two quilted strips 7×3 inches long. Lay them right side down on the work surface. Fold the entire length of the top and bottom edges of each strip ½ inch into the center. Hot-glue these folds in place

and hot-glue a 7-inch length of ribbon along the center of the band, trapping the folded edges and covering the remaining wrong side of the quilted backing. Cut four 2-inch lengths of ribbon and then fold one over each end of the wristband. Hot-glue them in place so they neatly cover the fabric ends. Glue a 2-inch section of loop fastener to each end of the wristbands. Trim the wristbands by gluing foliage and butterflies onto the

right inside of the finished bands.

3 To make the hat, hot-glue pieces of moss to the underside, outer edge, and top of the hat brim. Cut branches of foliage off the bushes and glue to hat. Continue gluing branches and moss until the hat is disguised. Position the nests, eggs, and birds

onto the branches and then glue them in place.

pearl skeletons

Made from ghost-white pearls, this may be the prettiest skeleton you'll ever meet. Using the diagram, *opposite*, you'll master beading on wire and have one made in no time. Kids love making this friendly fellow, too, so be sure to gather enough supplies for everyone to join in the fun.

supplies

Wire cutters
24-gauge silver
  beading wire
3- or 4-mm pearl
  beads
Jump rings
Scissors
Black ribbon

what to do

1 Cut a 3-foot length of wire and fold it in half. Hold both ends as you work.

2 Begin threading the first row of the diagram, a pearl followed by a jump ring and two more pearls. Let these beads fall to the center of the wire. Next follow the second row of the diagram, stringing four pearls onto one wire end. Thread the other wire end through all four beads in the opposite direction and then tightly pull both ends. You should now have two rows of pearls, one laying over the other. Continue working in this fashion, following the chart until you reach the arms.

3 Each arm is strung on a single wire. Thread five arm beads followed by three finger beads. String the wire back through the five arm beads so that the finger beads form a loop at the end of the arm. Repeat the process for the second arm using the second wire. Continue following the diagram, passing both wires through each row of beads until the legs are reached.

4 The legs are strung individually the same way as for the arms. String

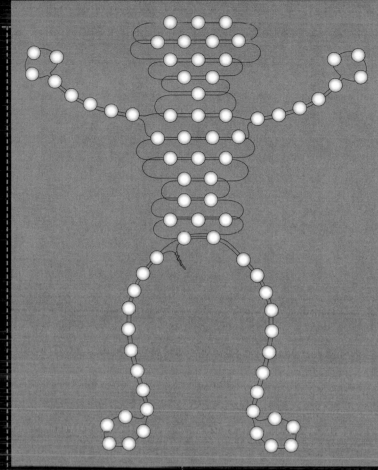

PEARL SKELETON BEADING DIAGRAM

nine beads for the leg itself and five beads for the foot. Thread the wire end back through the nine leg beads and then through the last row of the body. Once the second leg is complete, twist the wire ends together and cut excess wire.

5 Cut ribbon 10 inches longer than desired. Thread ribbon end through jump ring. Place around neck and tie ends into a bow.

COOL DUDE GIRL MASK PATTERNS

1 SQUARE = 1 INCH

COOL DUDE BOY MASK PATTERNS   **1 SQUARE = 1 INCH**

ghostly jewelry

Get in the Halloween spirit with these gliding ghosts that would rather hang out with you than rattle any chains.

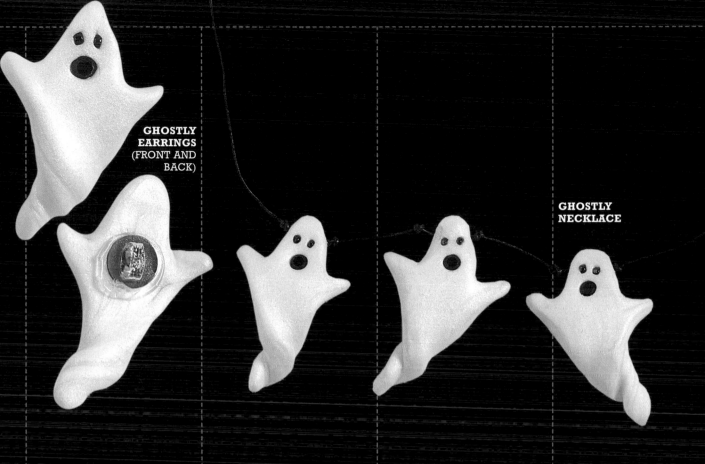

GHOSTLY
EARRINGS
(FRONT AND
BACK)

GHOSTLY
NECKLACE

supplies

**Pearlescent white
polymer clay**
**Flat-back black
rhinestones**
Black seed beads
**Toothpick or
darning needle**
**Thin black
leather cord**
Earring backs
**Strong adhesive,
such as E6000**

what to do

1 Work the clay
in your hands
to make it warm
and pliable. Form a
ghost with a ¾-inch
ball of clay. Pinch
the top into a flat,
rounded point;
then pinch out two
small arms from
the sides. Flatten
the center and then
lengthen the
remaining clay so
it ends in a point.

Twist the pointed
end under and
around to give
the bottom a
swirling effect.
2 Press the
rhinestone
mouth and seed
bead eyes in place.
For necklace
pieces, pierce a
darning needle or
toothpick sideways
through the top of
the ghost to make
holes for stringing.

3 Bake according
to package
instructions.
Thread pierced
ghosts onto the
leather cord, tying
knots in the cord to
separate the
ghosts. Glue
remaining ghosts
to earring backs.
Let the glue dry.

bouquet costumes

Let your little ones bloom as colorful garden flowers made from sheets of crafting foam.

forget-me-not

supplies
2 blue, 1 peach, and 1 green crafting foam sheets, such as Fun Foam
Scissors; ruler
Needle; thread
Fabric-covered headband
Paper punch
$\frac{1}{8}$-inch-wide ribbon

what to do
1 For blue petals, cut six heart-shape petals with flat bottoms, approximately $6\frac{1}{2}\times7\frac{1}{2}$ inches. For peach petals, cut nine petals, $2\frac{1}{2}\times2\frac{1}{2}$ inches. For green leaves, cut seven heart-shape leaves, $5\times6\frac{1}{2}$ inches. Cut two small leaves, 3×3 inches.

2 Place blue petals on the inside of the headband. Starting at one end, hand-stitch petal to edge of headband through both foam and cloth of the headband. Work another row of stitches halfway down the inside to keep the petal flat. Overlap the next petal by $1\frac{1}{2}$ inches and repeat until all petals are attached.

3 Stitch peach petals along the bottom of the headband, overlapping petals by $\frac{1}{4}$ inch.

4 For the collar, punch two holes at top of each leaf, about $1\frac{1}{2}$ inches apart. Thread ribbon through holes.

morning glory

supplies
2 dark pink, 1 light pink, and 2 green crafting foam sheets, such as Fun Foam

Scissors; ruler
Needle; thread
Small straw hat,
  pink if available
Paper punch
4 fat, pink
  chenille stems

3 fat, green
  chenille stems
1/8-inch-wide
  ribbon

what to do

1 For dark pink petals, cut four petals, $8\frac{1}{2}\times11$ inches. For light pink petals, cut four petals $5\frac{1}{2}\times7$ inches, and four petal strips 2×7 inches. For stem top, cut a green 13-inch starburst (see photo, *below*). Remove a triangular section from the starburst pattern, about $\frac{1}{4}$ of the circle. For collar leaves, cut four heart-shape leaves $6\frac{1}{2}\times8\frac{1}{2}$ inches. Cut five small leaves $4\frac{1}{2}\times6$ inches.

2 Stitch flat end of large petals $1\frac{1}{2}$ inches apart around the outer base of turned-up hat brim. Stitch small petals between the large ones. Tack sides together to keep upright. Tack top and bottom of inner petals to center of large ones.

3 Fold pink chenille stems in half. Poke ends through back of hat and pull to front. Curl ends. Poke end of a green stem through top of hat. Twist end to secure.

4 Form stem top into cone and sew together. Place on hat top, pulling chenille stem through the top.

5 Punch two holes at top of each leaf. Thread ribbon through holes. Curl remaining green chenille stems and attach to leaves.

113

funny animal masks

Whether you want to pretend you're a pet or tweet like a bird, all of these animal masks are a hoot! Wear a coordinating sweat suit and you're ready to play the part.

fluffy and fido masks

supplies
Tracing paper
Pencil
Scissors
1 large sheet each of black and white crafting foam, such as Fun Foam
1 small sheet each of tan, red, dark pink, blue, green, and yellow crafting foam
Strong adhesive, such as E6000
Gem glue
Acrylic gems in purple and clear
Needle
Elastic thread

what to do
1 Enlarge and trace the patterns on pages 116–117. Cut out the patterns. Trace around the patterns on the crafting foam. Cut out the shapes.

2 Layer and glue the pieces in place. Let dry.

3 Using gem glue, adhere the gems on the cat's collar. Let dry.

4 Cut a 10-inch length of elastic thread and insert into needle. Secure one end of thread at temple area of the mask by making a small stitch and knotting the thread. Sew through opposite side of the mask, adjusting the thread to fit. Knot thread; trim.

hooty owl mask

supplies

Safety goggles, available at discount and home center stores; **2 old CDs**
Strong adhesive, such as **E6000**
Tracing paper
Pencil; scissors
1 small sheet each of black and yellow crafting foam, such as **Fun Foam**
Feathers

what to do

1 To determine the placement of the CDs, first put on the safety goggles mask. Look in a mirror and place the CDs over the goggles, adjusting to see in the center holes of the CDs. Remove from face and glue the CDs on the goggles.

2 Trace the patterns on *page 118.* Cut out the patterns. Trace around the patterns on the crafting foam. Cut out the shapes.

3 Glue the foam pieces on top of the CDs. Using the photo, *below,* as a guide, glue the feathers in place. Let dry.

funny feathers mask

supplies

Tracing paper
Pencil; scissors
Crafting foam in black, white, and yellow, such as **Fun Foam**
Thick white crafts glue
Eye mask
Red acrylic paint
Paintbrush
Hot-glue gun and glue sticks
Feather

what to do

1 Trace the patterns, *page 119.* Cut out and trace onto foam. Cut out shapes.

2 Using crafts glue, adhere the white eye pieces atop the black pieces. Lay the mask over the foam eyes and trace the eye holes. Cut out the holes.

3 Paint the mask red. Let dry.

4 Hot-glue the eyes onto the mask, aligning the eye holes.

5 Carefully score the center of the beak using scissors. Fold on the line and glue to the mask as shown, *below.*

6 Hot-glue the feather in place. Let the glue dry.

funny animal masks continued

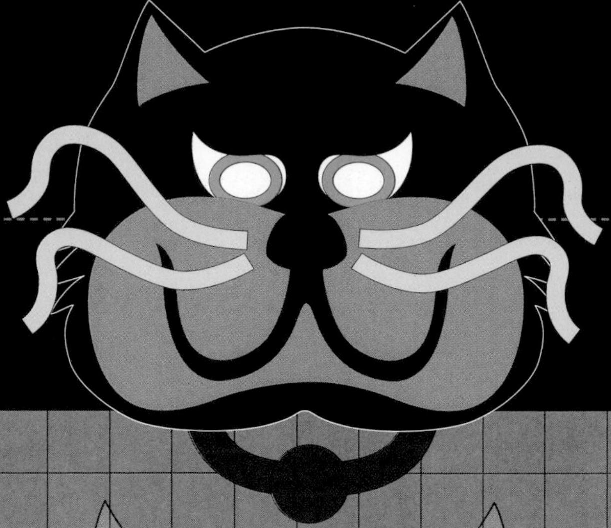

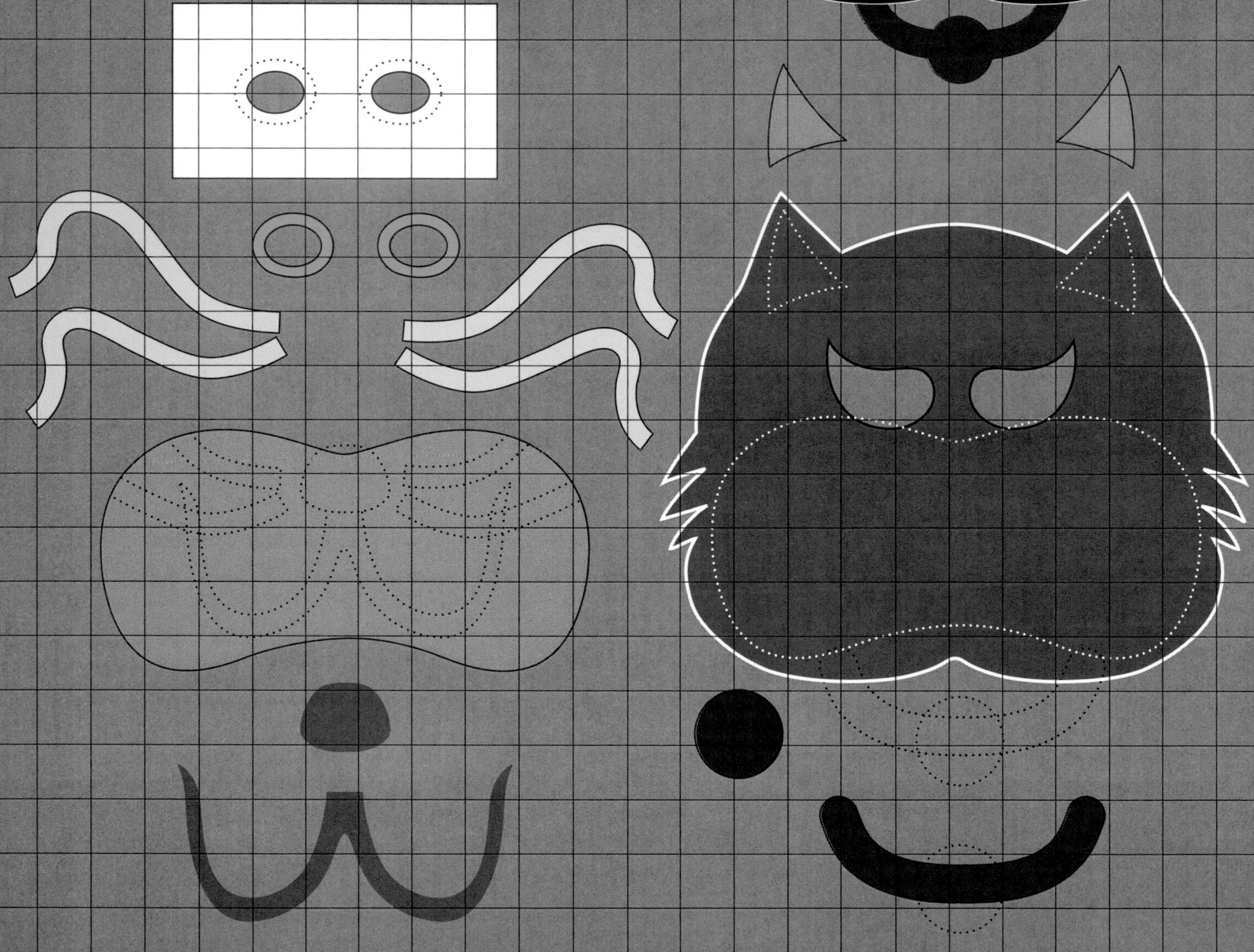

FLUFFY MASK PATTERNS

1 SQUARE = 1 INCH

FIDO MASK PATTERNS   1 SQUARE = 1 INCH

117

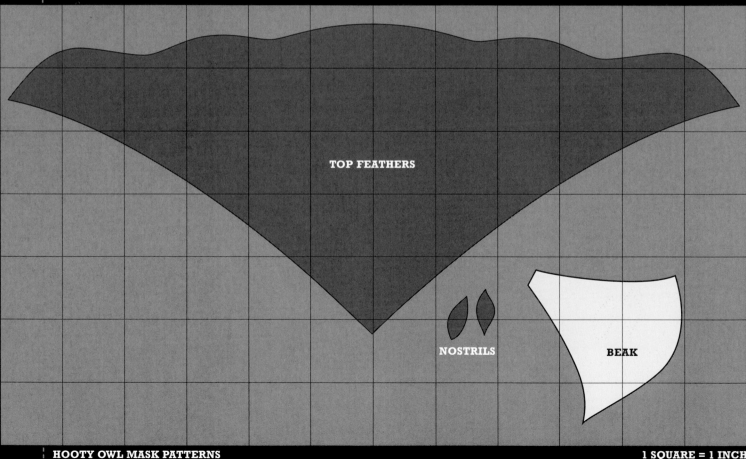

TOP FEATHERS

NOSTRILS

BEAK

HOOTY OWL MASK PATTERNS

1 SQUARE = 1 INCH

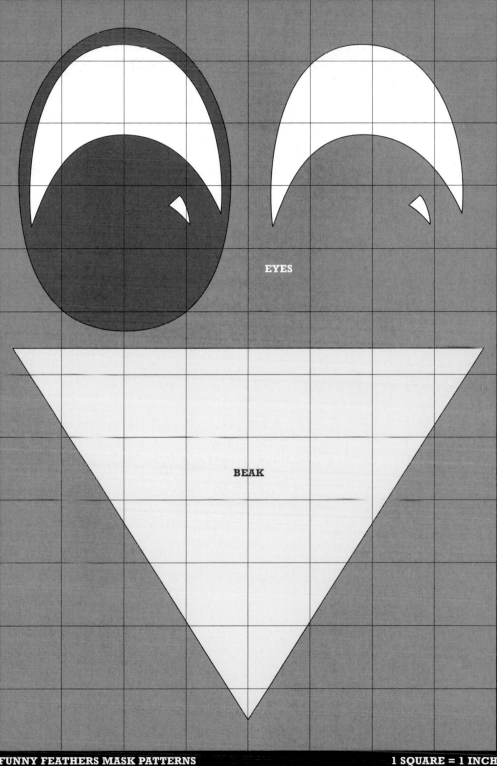

EYES

BEAK

jesting jester

You can't help but feel jolly with this jingling jester in your midst. The hat and collar are made from bright felt and the polka-dot stick has trailing ribbons with jingle-bell ends.

supplies

Tracing paper
Pencil
Scissors
Felt in turquoise, light orange, orange, bright pink, black, and purple
Pinking shears
Matching thread
Fiberfill; buttons
Straight pins
Child's sweatshirt
Purple cotton embroidery floss
Jingle bells
23-inch length of ¾-inch dowel
Paintbrush
2-inch wood doll head
Hot-glue gun and glue sticks
Acrylic paints in orange and black
2 yards of 1-inch-wide black and orange wire-edged ribbon

what to do

1 Enlarge and trace the patterns on *pages 122–123*. Cut out the patterns. Use the patterns to cut pieces from desired colors of felt with pinking shears.

2 To make the hat, layer the front and the back pieces. Using ¼-inch seams, sew the front and back sets together. Sew the left and right top pieces together.

To add the hatband, cut a 21×2½-inch piece from yellow felt. Sew the short ends together. Sew the band to the top piece. Sew buttons

where indicated on the pattern. Stuff the points of the hat with fiberfill.

3 To make the collar, pin the felt pieces in place, using the

photo, *opposite,* as a guide. Sew the felt pieces to the sweatshirt around the collar area with embroidery floss and small Xs. Tack the tips down by

sewing a jingle bell to each tip.

4 To make the jester's stick, glue the flat side of the wood ball to

continued on page 122

one end of the dowel. Paint the dowel orange and the ball black. Let the paint dry. To add polka dots, dip the eraser of a pencil into the paint and dot onto the surface. Let the paint dry. Cut the ribbon in half. Tie one ribbon length just below the ball on the stick. Knot in place. Tie the remaining ribbon above the first, tying the ends into a bow. To add a jingle bell to each ribbon end, pull both wires in each ribbon end to extend 1 inch beyond the ribbon. Twist the ends together. Insert the twisted wires into the loop in a jingle bell. Twist to secure. Repeat for all ribbon ends.

JESTER COLLAR PATTERN

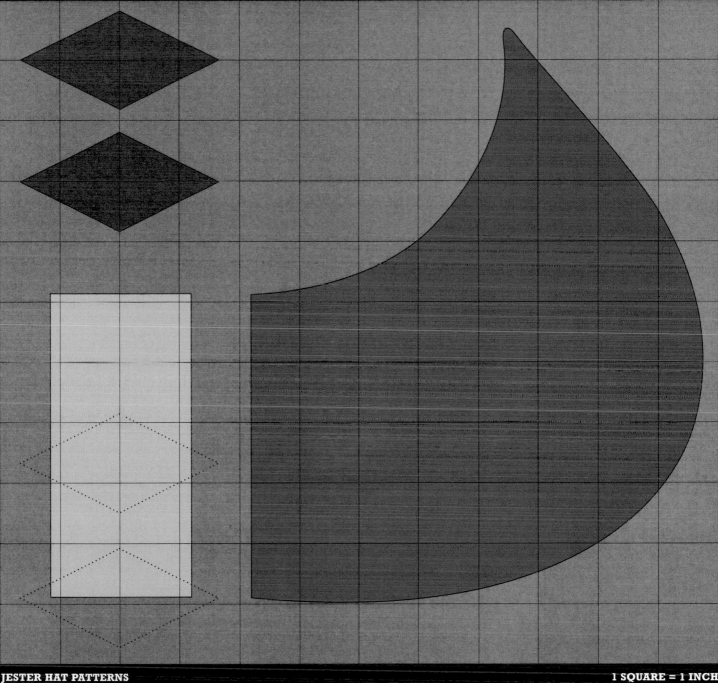

get ready

party ideas to concoct some fun

to celebrate

potion goblets

For a Halloween toast, raise these festive flutes filled with your favorite potion.

supplies
Clear glasses
  with long stems
Chenille stems in
  purple, orange,
  black, and
  lime green
Silver adhesive
  stars

what to do
1 Wash and dry the glasses. Beginning at the bottom of the stem, wrap tightly with a purple chenille stem. Continue wrapping the stem using the chenille stems as shown, *left.* When wrapping the top lime green chenille stem, wrap half of the length and then form the end into a spiral or zigzag shape.

2 Apply stars randomly to the outside of the glass top, avoiding the rim area. Remove the trims before washing the glass.

batty the lollipop holder

supplies
Tracing paper
Pencil
Construction paper in black, orange, white, and lime green
Scissors
Glue stick
Fine-point marking pens in black and silver
Large- and medium-size paper punches
Lollipop

what to do

1 Enlarge and trace the patterns and the hole positions, *right*. Cut out.

2 Trace around the bat shape on black paper, the banner on orange, and the fangs on white. Cut out the shapes. For the eyes, punch out two white circles using the large paper punch. Use the smaller punch to make a green nose. Glue the shapes into place.

3 Draw in the black and silver details and the lettering using marking pens. Fold the wings inward, as shown in the photo, *above*. Punch two holes in each wing as shown. Align the hole punches; then insert the lollipop stick through the holes.

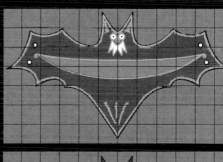

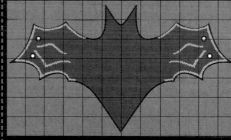

127

wizard hat ringtoss

Munchkins of all ages will love playing this game of skill at your next Halloween bash. The foam cone is glued atop a terra-cotta base for weight. Wrapped with trims of all kinds, the cone makes good use of odds and ends. Once the plastic-lid rings are cut out, let the kids wrap them with chenille stems in their favorite Halloween colors.

supplies

- 2-inch foam ball, such as Styrofoam
- Toothpick
- Thick white crafts glue
- 12-inch-high foam cone, such as Styrofoam
- 6-inch terra-cotta flowerpot saucer
- Hot-glue gun and glue sticks
- Cording in silver, gold, purple, black, and green
- Scissors; ruler
- Straight pins
- Ribbon in purple, black, green, and orange
- Silver sequins on a string
- 1½-inch star sequins
- Quilting pins
- Plastic lids from large margarine containers
- Chenille stems in orange, black, purple, silver, green, and gold

what to do

1. Press the foam ball against a hard, flat work surface to slightly flatten one side. Insert a toothpick halfway into the flattened side. Dab crafts glue on the flattened area of the ball and on the toothpick. Press into the top of the foam cone. Hot-glue the bottom of the cone to the bottom of the flowerpot saucer. Let dry.

2. Wrap the foam ball with silver cording, pinning the ends to secure. Wrap the saucer base with desired cording and ribbon using hot glue to adhere.

3. Cut 3-inch lengths from various widths of ribbon. Pin the ribbon pieces vertically at the bottom of the cone.

Continue wrapping the top of the cone using different colors of cording, silver sequin strings, and ribbon as desired.

4. Cut a 24-inch length of silver cording. Wrap the cording diagonally around the cone, shaping the ends into spirals. Pin in place. Use quilting pins to secure star sequins by the cording spirals and randomly on the cone.

5. To make a ring, carefully cut the rim off a plastic lid. Cut a circle from the center of the lid, leaving a 1-inch ring. Wrap the ring with the desired colors of chenille stems.

6. To play, have players try to toss their rings onto the wizard hat.

mummy bowling

A new twist on an old favorite, this wide-eyed mummy bowling set will have youngsters howling with delight.

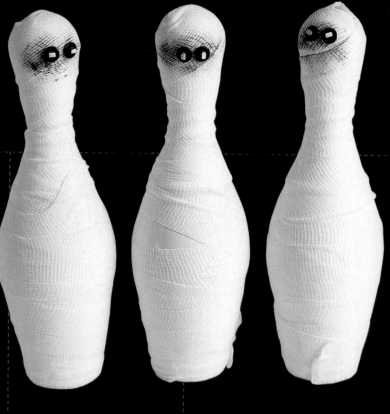

supplies

Plastic bowling set
White spray primer, optional
Black spray paint, optional
Scissors
20 yards of 2- to 3-inch-wide gauze bandage
Thick white crafts glue
Acrylic paints in green and orange
Paintbrush
¼-inch black buttons
Pencil with round eraser

what to do

1 If the bowling pins are colored, spray-paint white in a well-ventilated work area. If the ball is not black, spray-paint it with primer. Let the paint dry. Spray-paint the ball black. Let dry.

2 Cut ten 2-yard lengths of gauze bandage. For each bowling pin, glue one end of the gauze at the bottom of the pin. Wrap the gauze toward the top of the pin and back to the bottom, applying dabs of glue to secure. Let dry.

3 On the top of each pin, paint a green oblong oval for the shading behind the eyes. Let the paint dry. For eyes, glue two black buttons side by side over the green painted area. Let dry.

4 To make dots on the bowling ball, dip the eraser of a pencil into orange paint and dot onto the surface. Let the paint dry.

spider surprise boxes

Use these printed spider boxes as fun dice shakers or to store small game pieces. If giving them as a gift, be sure to tuck a piece or two of Halloween candy inside.

supplies
Rectangular
  plastic boxes
Glass cleaner
Paper towels
Black acrylic paint
Paper plate
Metallic pom-pom
Scrap paper
Black paint
  markers
Cotton swabs
Clear acrylic
  gloss sealer
Small wiggly eyes

Hot-glue gun and
  glue sticks
Small toys or
  candies

what to do
1 Remove labels and clean boxes with glass cleaner and paper towels.

2 Squeeze out a small amount of paint onto a paper plate. For the spider body, dip the pom-pom into the paint and test print it onto scrap paper. When pleased with the results, print directly onto box and lid where desired. Let the paint dry.

3 Use the paint marker to draw eight legs coming out of the printed body. To make a foot, dip the cotton swab end into the paint and test print it. Print a round foot at the end of each leg. Let the paint dry.

4 In a well-ventilated work area, spray a coat of sealer over the box. Let dry. Hot-glue two wiggly eyes onto the base of each printed pom-pom body. Let the glue dry. Fill the box with game pieces or Halloween surprises.

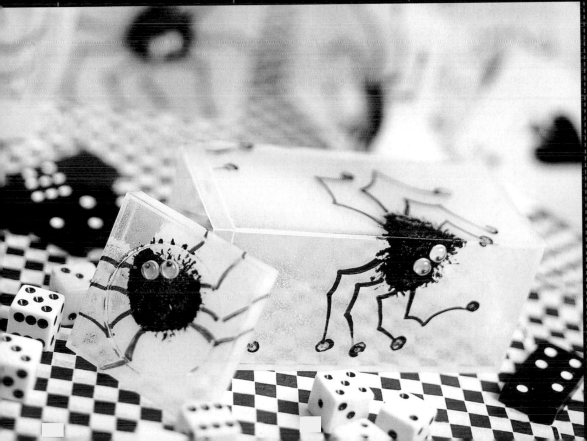

creepy candles

Enjoy the glow from canning jar luminarias. Black and white marbles and orange ribbon add Halloween flair.

supplies
Canning jar
Marbles in black and white
White votive candle
Scissors
1-inch-wide orange-and-black wire-edged ribbon
Yardstick

what to do
1 Wash and dry the canning jar. Fill the jar one-third full with black and white marbles. Nestle a votive candle in the center of the marbles.

2 Cut an 18-inch length of ribbon. Tie around the top of the jar. Trim the ribbon ends.

Note: Never leave burning candles unattended.

crystal ball bowl

A party-time favorite, fortune-telling is all the more fun with this bowl of mystery at hand. Write several fortunes so each guest can take one home.

supplies

Glass bowl
Bubble Magic glue
Paintbrush
White or black tissue paper
Iridescent fine glitter
White or black paint marker
Acrylic spray sealer
Black or white tissue or crepe paper and contrasting markers
Pinking shears
Ruler

what to do

1 Squeeze Bubble Magic into the bowl and use a paintbrush to spread the glue to cover the inside of the bowl. Tear sections of tissue paper and lay them over the glue. Gently run your fingers over the back of the tissue to squeeze out any air bubbles. Brush more Bubble Magic over the tissue paper to firmly adhere it to the glass. Continue working in this manner until two-thirds of the glass is covered, randomly leaving clear openings on the bowl.

2 Shake glitter into the bowl and then cover the opening with your hand. Rotate the bowl with the other hand to distribute the glitter. While the glue is drying, draw question marks on the outside of the glass with a paint marker. If you make a mistake, you can wipe it off with paint thinner, clean the surface, and start again.

3 In a well-ventilated area, spray two to three coats of sealer inside the bowl to help secure the glitter. Let the sealer dry.

4 Cut $1/2 \times 4$-inch paper strips using pinking shears. Write fortunes on paper.

jester goody sacks

Styled after a jester's hat, this felt sack is big enough to hold a tasty treasure.

supplies
Tracing paper
Pencil
Scissors
Felt in orange and black
Matching thread
Beading needle
Large seed beads in white and orange
Small seed beads in orange and black
Black rococo beads
White cotton embroidery floss
Sewing needle
White pony beads
Round black beads

what to do

1 Trace the pattern, *opposite,* and cut it out. Trace around pattern twice on orange felt and twice on black felt. Cut out shapes.

2 On the bottom section of a black felt piece, sew on large white seed beads secured by small orange seed beads. Thread needle with thread. Knot ends. From back side, push needle through black felt. Thread on a white seed bead and an orange seed bead. Push needle back through the white seed bead and into the felt. Continue adding beads randomly in this manner until the bottom portion of the felt piece is sprinkled with beads below the fold line. Repeat for the other black felt shape.

3 Flip the black piece over and add short lengths of orange seed beads to the top section. From the back (right side), push a threaded needle through the felt. String on four

seed beads. Push needle back through felt, making a short row of seed beads. Continue adding random designs in this manner until the top portion is covered. Repeat for the other black felt shape.

4 Add beads to the orange felt pieces in the same manner. For the bottoms, sew on rococo beads. For tops, sew on small black seed beads.

5 To connect pieces, join the sides and bottom points with wrong sides together. Use an even whipstitch and two plies of floss to join an orange felt piece to a black felt piece below the fold as shown, *right.* Whipstitch the seam a second time, crossing the

first threads to make an X. Sew all seams in this manner until all four pieces are joined. Flip the points down. Sew a pony bead, a round black bead, and a large orange seed bead to each point.

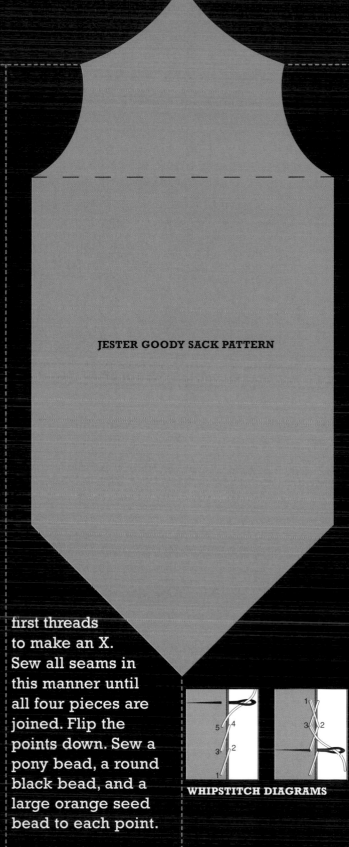

JESTER GOODY SACK PATTERN

WHIPSTITCH DIAGRAMS

Made from a papier-mâché-covered balloon, this piñata holds a pumpkin full of treats behind her smile.

supplies
- 15-inch balloon
- 2 medium bowls
- 3 cups white flour
- Water
- Newspapers
- Scissors
- Crafts knife
- Tracing paper
- Pencil
- Medium-weight colored paper in black, purple, yellow, and orange
- Glue stick
- Party hat in metallic blue or other desired color
- Paper punch
- Silver eyelets and eyelet tool
- Lime green plastic lace
- Yardstick
- 2 yards of ¼-inch-wide ribbon
- Darning needle
- Crepe paper streamers in orange and green
- Small candies or plastic Halloween toys

piñata

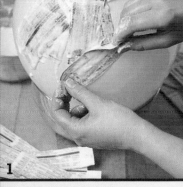

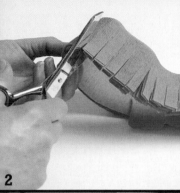

what to do

1 Inflate the balloon and secure with a knot. Set the balloon in one of the bowls.

2 To make papier-mâché mixture, pour flour into remaining bowl. Add water until the mixture has the consistency of thick gravy.

3 Tear newspapers into strips. Using one strip at a time, dip the strip into the flour mixture. Gently pull the strip between two fingers to remove excess mixture. Place wet strip on balloon as shown in Photo 1, *right*. Continue adding strips to the balloon in this manner until the exposed balloon is covered with two to three layers of paper, leaving the balloon knot exposed. Turn the balloon over in the bowl and repeat. Let dry. Remove balloon from bowl. Holding the balloon by the knot, puncture the balloon and remove from the hardened papier-mâché shape.

4 Enlarge and trace the patterns, *pages 140–141*. Cut out patterns. Trace around patterns on colored paper. Cut out shapes. Trace around one eye pattern on small end of balloon in eye area. Use a crafts knife to cut out eye shape, ¼ inch inside the drawn line.

5 Glue the black pieces on the yellow eyes and the purple stripes on the hands and legs. Cut a 10-inch circle from black paper for the hat brim.

Place the party hat in the center of the paper circle. Trace the party hat. Cut out slightly inside the circle. Glue the party hat to the brim. Let dry.

6 Using the pattern as a guide, punch holes along the tops of both shoes. Use an eyelet tool to secure eyelets in each hole as shown, *opposite*. Cut two 24-inch lengths of lime green lace. Lace through eyelets and tie ends into a bow. Glue shoes onto bottom of legs. Let the glue dry.

7 Use a crafts knife to cut two small holes in the top of the piñata. Insert ribbon into needle. Sew through holes in piñata top. Remove the needle. Knot the ribbon ends to secure.

8 Cut 4 yards of crepe paper at a time. Wrap paper into a 1-foot loop. Carefully cut ½-inch-wide fringes along one side of the loop, being careful not to trim through the edges as shown in Photo 2, *above*.

continued on page 140

9 Beginning at the bottom (large end) of the papier-mâché shape, wind and glue unfringed edge to the shape as shown in Photo 3, *page 139.* Continue wrapping and gluing until the shape is covered. Through the eye opening, fill the piñata with candy or toys.

10 Pleat the arms. Glue the paper pieces onto the fringe-covered shape, making sure to cover cutout eye area with a paper eye. Let dry.

11 Tie a bow from green crepe paper. Glue onto hat. Let dry. Thread hanging loop through tip of hat.

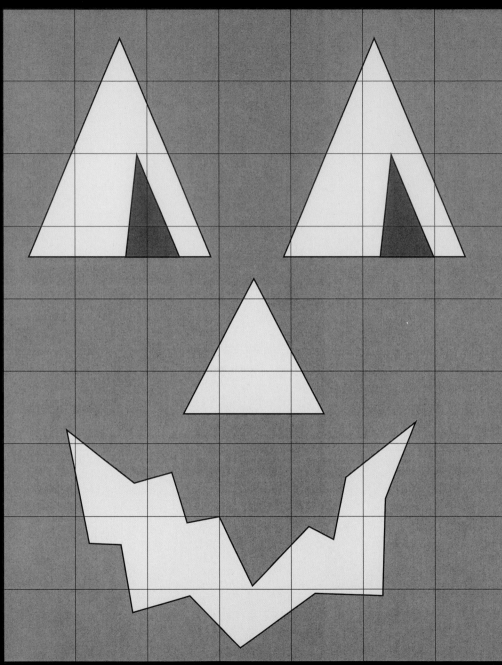

JUMPIN' JACK-O'-LANTERN FACE PATTERNS
1 SQUARE = 1 INCH

index